Jo D9C6:

I do hope you enjoy this story about the early years of Tennis in America — from a different perspective.

[signature]

09/29/09

Whirlwind

The Godfather of Black Tennis

Whirlwind at 19.

The Life and Times of Dr. Robert Walter Johnson

By Doug Smith

BLUE EAGLE PUBLISHING COMPANY, LLC
WASHINGTON, D.C.

Whirlwind: The Life and Times of Dr. Robert Walter Johnson

Copyright © 2004 by Doug Smith. All rights reserved.
No portion of this book, except for brief review, may be reproduced,
stored in a retrieval system or transmitted in any form or by any means—
electronic, mechanical, photocopying, recording, or otherwise—
without written permission of the publisher.
For information contact Blue Eagle Publishing, LLC.

Published by Blue Eagle Publishing, LLC
601 G. St. SW
Washington, D.C. 20024

Cover design by Jerome Smith of BrandEvolve and Garrett Brown of Opaque
Design and Print Production

Printed in the United States of America

To contact Blue Eagle Publishing, visit our website at
www.blueeaglepublishing.com

Library of Congress Cataloging-in-Publication Data

Smith, Doug, 1942–
Whirlwind: The Godfather of Black Tennis / by Doug Smith
ISBN 0-9748111-0-6 (cloth)
ISBN 0-9748111-1-4 (pbk.)

To my wife, Anne, whose unwavering love and support cleared the way for the resurrection of a project long abandoned. . . . .

And to my sons, Jerome and Jared, who pitched in without being pestered to do so.

Table of Contents

Dedication		III
Foreword		VII
Acknowledgements		IX
Introduction		XI
Chapter 1	The Charlottesville Challenge	1
Chapter 2	Family	7
Chapter 3	Out of Control	14
Chapter 4	Whirlwind	19
Chapter 5	A Coaching Phase	26
Chapter 6	A New Wife	32
Chapter 7	Small Town Doctor	36
Chapter 8	History of the ATA	42
Chapter 9	Other Loves	48
Chapter 10	Aiding Althea	55
Chapter 11	The Good Life	64
Chapter 12	Junior Development	70
Chapter 13	The California Kid	78
Chapter 14	Lessons in Humility	83
Chapter 15	A Disruptive Feud	93
Chapter 16	King Arthur	98
Chapter 17	Victory at Charlottesville	103
Chapter 18	You Go, Girls	109

CONTENTS

Chapter 19	New Attitude	115
Chapter 20	Father-Daughter	120
Chapter 21	Father-Son	126
Chapter 22	Dr. El	133
Chapter 23	Juan	138
Chapter 24	Last Reward	144
Chapter 25	Ten Feet Tall	150
Epilogue		159
Bonus Chapter		171
Apppendix A		179
Appendix B		181

Foreword

I BECAME AWARE OF Dr. Robert Walter Johnson's impact as a tennis guru in the 1970s when I played one of his protégés, Juan Farrow, who was the nation's top-ranked player among 12-year-olds in 1970 and 14s in 1972.

Big for his age, Juan ruled the younger junior divisions, combining toughness and tenacity with ferocious ground strokes. We clashed several times as juniors and Juan claims that his final win against me occurred in the 18s division, about a month before I streaked to stardom by reaching the 1977 Wimbledon semifinals. Juan, you cannot be serious! Someone will have to show me a replay before I'll buy that.

Earlier, when I played Juan in the 12s, I saw this elderly black man sitting in the stands, cheering for him. I learned later that that same man had developed and guided the early careers of hundreds of promising young black players, including Althea Gibson and Arthur Ashe, who became two of the game's most disciplined and popular champions.

A gifted athlete, Althea played my kind of game—serve-and-volley—with incomparable fluidity and style, and Arthur, my Davis Cup captain for several years, became a good friend and an inspiration as a tennis spokesman and international leader. In his autobiography, *Days of Grace,* Arthur said he began to see me as a brother, but then he spoiled it a bit by adding that I was in some ways an incorrigible brother. Hey, it's tough to dispute that. Arthur and I had our differences, even our clashes, but I had a huge amount of respect for him as a man, a black man and a positive force for world tennis. I realized too late that he was the greatest ambassador our sport had ever had, and I am determined to try to do better myself.

Helping to put an overdue spotlight on Dr. Johnson, a major contributor to the tennis world, is another way I can make a meaningful contribution to the game I love. At a time when blacks were barred

FOREWORD

from competing in USTA-sanctioned tennis events, Dr. Johnson moved quietly but firmly to convince the powers-to-be to change their ways. He didn't bang on doors, like I might have done. Instead, he rapped politely, spoke calmly and urged each white tournament director to allow his juniors the opportunity to be the best that they could be. Many of them did.

For more than 20 years, Dr. Johnson recruited the best black juniors in the country to train under his guidance on a tennis court that he built in the backyard of his Lynchburg, Va. home. Along with the rules of tennis, he taught the rules of life. Etiquette, honesty, sportsmanship and self-control were among Dr. Johnson's litany of daily lessons. Okay, I might have had trouble getting into Dr. Johnson's camp and not just because I didn't have the right skin color.

Armed only with an engaging smile and steely resolve, Dr. Johnson never wavered from his goal. More than once, Althea and Arthur conceded that without Dr. Johnson, they never would have become the first black players to win major tennis titles.

Needless to say, our sport, our country, indeed the world community, became a better place because of Althea and Arthur's achievements. Dr. Johnson made it possible for them to succeed. His extraordinary role should be remembered, appreciated and applauded not just by African Americans but also by everyone who strives for equality and justice.

Like most of us, Dr. Johnson made his share of mistakes in his lifetime. Who hasn't? But his pros far outweigh his cons. Clearly, he deserves long overdue accolades from the world tennis community. Let's start by creating a major contributor's spot for him at the International Tennis Hall of Fame in Newport, RI. His was a special life and he deserves the honor.

John McEnroe

Acknowledgments

Though it took a while to complete—more than 20 years—I can't think of anything I've written that's more personally gratifying than *'Whirlwind.'*

Now let me fess up. It *didn't* really take 20 years to write. After my first attempt to tell Robert Walter Johnson's life story fell through in early 1983, I stored it in the back of my mind. There it languished for nearly 19 years. After retiring from *USA Today* in the fall of 2001, I retrieved the dusty manuscript from a box in a closet and spent the next six months, updating and massaging it. I also found a few other voices to help tell the story.

Much of the research for *Whirlwind* was accomplished during a six-month leave of absence from my job as editor of publications at Howard University Hospital in 1982. In gathering data for this book, I made several trips to cities along the East Coast and talked to more than 200 people who knew Dr. Johnson at various stages of his life.

I made three trips to Plymouth, North Carolina, where Dr. Johnson spent most of his formative years and to Lynchburg, Virginia, where he established a medical practice and conducted his groundbreaking tennis camp for juniors. I also visited Lincoln University in Pennsylvania, where the legend of 'Whirlwind' was born. I tracked down and interviewed several of Dr. Johnson's Lincoln classmates. His relatives invited me into their homes and shared both precious and painful memories of a man they loved dearly. I am especially grateful to Dr. Johnson's now deceased sisters—Victoria Bonds, Eva Cooper and Dr. Eileen El Dorado Johnson—and two of his children—Robert Walter Johnson Jr. and Carolyn Waltee Moore.

I thank Jake Wells and Edgar Lee for allowing me to use their copies of programs that were distributed each year at the American Tennis Association (ATA) National Championships. Whirlwind often used the

ACKNOWLEDGMENTS

ATA programs to explain his progress with the camp. I used some of Whirlwinds messages and photos to help tell his story and I'm grateful to the ATA for allowing me to do that. I am grateful to the late Bertram Baker, a former executive secretary of the ATA, and Clifford Blackman for sharing their thoughts and experiences.

Ed Fabricius, media relations director of the United States Tennis Association (USTA) in the 1970s and early '80s, granted me access to early USTA files and tournament records, including the U.S. Tennis Championships. A. J. Barnes, a former editor with *Black Tennis* magazine, also provided special assistance.

Alice Burnette, who first began improving my writing skills when we were classmates in junior high school, improved the manuscript with corrections and insightful suggestions. I thank Robert Robinson, deputy managing editor of sports at *USA Today,* and Dr. Robert M. Screen, Hampton University professor, for their recommendations and input. I'm grateful, too, that Andre Christopher, *Tennis Week*'s managing editor, agreed to do the final edit. Thanks Andre, for a masterful job.

When Whirlwind was just an idea, *Washington Post* columnist Tony Kornheiser shared my belief that *Whirlwind* was a project worth doing. He encouraged me to stay the course, despite the setbacks. Thanks a bunch, Anthony.

About a year ago, my younger son, Jared, decided that the best way to keep his dad from going bonkers over the book was to find a publisher. Alas, he volunteered for the job. My other son, Jerome, a graphic designer, took charge of the visuals. Thus it became a family project and I'm quite proud of what the Smith family has produced.

I've saved special thanks for my wife, Anne, who has provided much love, happiness and support during the development of this project, which she has made her own. A few years ago, she vowed that *Whirlwind* would be published even if it meant investing a portion of our retirement funds to the project. And so we did.

Introduction

In the summer of 1960, I spent two of the most exciting weeks of my teenaged years at the Lynchburg, Virginia, home of Dr. Robert Walter (Whirlwind) Johnson, who trained promising black juniors on his backyard tennis court.

I first learned of Dr. Johnson and his tennis camp for talented black juniors in 1958 when I was a 15-year-old sophomore at George P. Phenix High School in Hampton, Virginia. Rufus Gant, my junior varsity basketball coach and varsity tennis coach, often spoke admiringly of this fabulously rich black doctor. Gant told us that for the past few years, Johnson had invited the best black juniors to his home, where he trained them and then took them to play in several integrated tournaments, including the USLTA Interscholastic Championships in Charlottesville, Virginia.

It was a time in our history when America consisted of two societies—one black, one white—and when blacks and whites, especially in the South, moved about in totally different worlds even when they lived in the same neighborhoods. By law, the races attended separate schools, drank from separate public water fountains, sat in separate sections at movie theatres and were treated in separate hospitals. Sometimes blacks, needing emergency care, died because they were refused admission to white hospitals. Sometimes whites, needing emergency care, died because they refused to be treated at a nearer black hospital. Ironically, relatives of those who died—black or white—asked the same Christian God to provide in heaven what their departed loved ones rarely shared on earth: peace and justice for all.

Like most black teachers of my era, Gant managed to keep images of success dancing in the minds of his black students despite the obstacles. He encouraged us to push ourselves beyond the limits imposed by racist policies and frequently reminded us that we must be twice as good

INTRODUCTION

as our white competitors. "Rejection might come even when you prove yourself, but never stop trying," Gant often said.

I really wasn't too enthused about learning to play tennis, which was considered to be—by guys in my neighborhood—"a sport for sissies." Baseball was the game that I yearned to play. But Gant maneuvered me to the tennis court, stuck a racket in my hand and the love match was on. Two years later, I was Phenix's No. 1 tennis player and Virginia's second best black player. What happened on my way to No. 1, you ask? I had trouble with this wiry fellow from Richmond's Maggie Walker High. But hey, a lot of players had trouble while facing Arthur Ashe on a tennis court. Arthur beat me 6-4, 6-0 in the 1960 Negro State High School Championships. A week later in Greensboro, North Carolina, he whipped me again (6-3, 6-2) in the semifinals of the Negro National Interscholastic Championships. By reaching the semifinals of the black national event, I automatically qualified for Dr. Johnson's junior development program and a berth in the USLTA Interscholastic Championships.

The next week, James Bryant Jr., my high school doubles partner, and I rode a Greyhound bus to Lynchburg. I don't remember how Jimmy was selected. Gant might have recommended him or maybe Jimmy's father, James Sr., then business manager at Hampton Institute (now Hampton University), used his political clout. Regardless, Jimmy helped make the adventure a tad more exciting.

After being assigned to our rooms, we were instructed to put on our tennis gear and loosen up on the court. Dr. Johnson wanted to get a look at us as soon as he got home from the office. I had neither met nor seen a photo of Dr. Johnson, but my experience growing up in the segregated South had conditioned me to expect a light-skinned black with wavy or curly hair, who spoke with a quiet but authoritative school master's voice. More often than not, those were the traits of an HNIC—Head Negro in Charge. I was right about the voice.

The dark brown-skinned man had thin gray hair, stood about 5'11" and weighed a solid 175 pounds. Wearing a white T-shirt, white pants and tennis shoes, he greeted us with firm handshakes, asked about our bus ride, and then directed us to the other side of the net. "Let's see what you've got," he said. Though nearly 61, Whirlwind moved about the

INTRODUCTION

court on younger legs. He hit balls to us alternately, testing our forehands and backhands. Neither Jimmy nor I kept the ball in play for more than five consecutive strokes and I'm not sure why we played so poorly. He dismissed us with a quizzical look and said, "You boys must be tired from your trip. We'll see what you look like after you've rested."

Joe Williams, of Durham, North Carolina, Thomas Hawes, of Wilmington, North Carolina, and John McGill, of Louisville, Kentucky, were the other male juniors at the camp. Whirlwind left us a list of practice drills and conditioning exercises to perform daily and we didn't dare deviate from his list. Each of us also was assigned daily chores. I swept the kitchen floor after breakfast, took out the trash, cut grass and helped water the courts. Once the court was rolled, we took turns practicing serves and overheads. Our sessions were unsupervised because Dr. Johnson went to his medical office each morning and rarely returned before 5 p.m.

In the evenings, he'd monitor our practice sets, correct us when he saw flaws and applaud our good shots. We often talked tennis at the dinner table, but we also received etiquette lessons. "Always scoop your soup away from you, and then bring the spoon to your mouth," he said. "I want you boys to be gentlemen and to watch your table manners when we're in Charlottesville next week. Don't act crazy and give these white folks an excuse not to let you play or invite us back."

Except for Dr. Johnson's group, the participants in the annual high school event, held each year on the campus of the University of Virginia, were white. Like some of the other guys, I never felt confident about playing white boys, primarily because I figured they had many more years of experience on the tennis court than I did. Dr. Johnson sensed our doubts and often provided confidence boosts during training. He made it clear, too, that in Charlottesville our behavior would be scrutinized as carefully as our skills on the court. In the car on the way to Charlottesville, he recited a litany of things for us not to do. Chief among them: We were not to question calls or argue about anything and we were not to swear or curse.

He wanted us to be focused but not too intense, confident but not too aggressive, relaxed but not inattentive. Bottom line, he also wanted very much for us to win. During the drive, he turned to me and said,

INTRODUCTION

"Arthur speaks very highly of you, says you're a smart player and that you played him tough in the state finals. Play like you did against him and you'll do okay. Don't be afraid."

In the first round, I faced a lanky redhead from Philadelphia who needed only 35 minutes to turn me into a spectator. The redhead crushed me 6-1, 6-1. Williams, McGill and Hawes didn't get much further in the draw and Arthur, the No. 8 seed, lost to top seed and eventual champion Bill Lenoir, of Tucson, Arizona, in the quarterfinals. The Ashe vs. Lenoir match will be discussed further in Chapter 16.

The following weekend, Dr. Johnson took Arthur and Joe to play in an integrated event; Hawes and I went to Norfolk, Virginia, to play in a tournament sanctioned by the predominantly black American Tennis Association (ATA). I had accepted a full tennis scholarship at Hampton Institute and Herman Neilson, Hampton's tennis coach, had gotten me a nine-week job at a camp in Bear Mountain, New York. Though I didn't spend but three weeks with Dr. Johnson's team—one traveling to tournaments—I left favorably impressed with what the good doctor was doing. For two weeks, I enjoyed the comforts of his home, three square meals per day and the best training conditions available for juniors anywhere. During that time, I had rackets restrung, got new shoes, new socks, new shirts or shorts and always played with fuzzy balls, something rarely seen during high school practice sessions.

I left Dr. Johnson's camp grateful for the opportunity and with many fond memories. But my desire to document Dr. Johnson's life evolved nearly 20 years later, in the summer of 1978, when I rediscovered the ATA. Laid off by the *New York Post* after a two-year stint, I returned to competitive tennis. The late Andrew Ferguson, a dear friend, and I spent the summer traveling the ATA circuit. We played in ATA events in New Haven, Connecticut; New York, East Orange, New Jersey; Philadelphia; and Washington, D.C., and ended the tour at Princeton University, site of the ATA National Championships.

I met top ATA players, George Stewart, Billy Davis, Edgar Lee and others I had heard about as a junior, but had never seen in action. I got reacquainted with old friends and established many new friendships. At social events and during other gatherings, we talked often of the history of the black tennis player. Invariably, the conversation would focus on

INTRODUCTION

the generous, demanding black physician, who helped guide several black players, including Hall of Fame champions Althea Gibson and Arthur Ashe, to prominence in tennis. Thanks to Dr. Johnson, more than 100 black juniors earned college scholarships during that era.

My respect for and curiosity about the black physician grew stronger after realizing that he had—mainly with his own funds—operated the junior development program for 20 years, until his death in 1971. Clearly, no one had matched Dr. Johnson's commitment to developing promising black juniors. Making money was never his motivation; guiding blacks to the highest level was his only goal. By producing top-ranked black juniors, he made his presence felt on the predominantly white USLTA junior circuit and became the tennis world's premier civil rights pioneer. Moreover, Dr. Johnson's junior development program was a prelude to the high-tech, junior training academies/camps, such as those run by tennis gurus Nick Bollettieri and Rick Macci and former champion Chris Evert.

Dr. Johnson's legacy represents a major contribution not only to blacks but also to tennis lovers everywhere. His name and his contributions deserve to be eternally preserved at the International Tennis Hall of Fame in Newport, Rhode Island.

Sharing Robert Walter Johnson's achievements and experiences with others by documenting his life story is my way of paying tribute to one of many unsung black heroes in American history.

1

The Charlottesville Challenge

WHILE DRIVING THROUGH Charlottesville, Virginia, the midway point of a Washington, D.C., to Lynchburg, Virginia, trip, Dr. Robert Walter Johnson noticed a sign near the entrance to the University of Virginia campus promoting a tennis tournament. Tennis fanatic that he was, Johnson couldn't resist stopping to take a look.

The sign, which read "Interscholastic Tennis Championships," guided him to the campus tennis courts, where he saw scores of white boys—dressed in white shorts and shirts—scrambling about the courts, slapping tennis balls at one another. He parked his green Buick near a fence on that warm, sunny day in June 1950, climbed out and leaned against the fence and gazed admiringly at the youngsters at play.

He noticed that the boys—without a single exception—swept their rackets back before striking the ball from either side, forehand or backhand. Each of them stroked the ball with second-natured ease down the line, then crosscourt. He watched some of them hit lobs—high arching shots—while their playing partners returned the lobs with overhead smashes. He noted the sureness in their footwork and steadiness in their arms and hands, as they rushed the net after serves, punching the ball before it bounced. Years later, he described them to be fundamentally sound, disciplined, focused and confident.

A self-taught player, Johnson at the time was tournament director of the Central Intercollegiate Athletic Association (CIAA), a group of black colleges that included Howard University and Hampton Institute. He suspected that the CIAA's best black collegian would finish a distant second against any of the white teens competing at the Charlottesville tournament, which was sponsored by the United States Lawn Tennis Association (USLTA).

"To my surprise, the caliber of play in high school there was better than our colleges—frankly better than the best tennis we Negroes had to offer anywhere in the United States," Johnson said. However, he saw no reason why younger, talented blacks, with the proper training and attitude, could not soon be competing in the same event. "I therefore decided to see what steps could be taken to get *our* boys in this national championship."

Johnson implemented his plan at a time when logic, fairness, decency and a sense of justice eluded many white Americans—especially Southerners—whenever they saw non-white skin. So strong was the South's desire to keep black Americans out of its mainstream, that the gatekeepers at many of its universities and colleges routinely denied intellectually gifted young blacks an opportunity to fulfill their potential, not caring that their potential might one day lead to discoveries that might benefit all humans.

There was, however, a steady breeze of change drifting through the land. A few white leaders already had made decisions that surely hastened the end of government-endorsed racial oppression. In 1947, major league baseball got its first black ballplayer when Brooklyn Dodgers general manager Branch Rickey signed Jackie Robinson. A year later, President Harry Truman, deciding that blacks in the military ought to enjoy the same respect, privileges and freedom as whites, integrated the nation's armed forces. Months earlier, Dr. Ralph Bunche became the first black to win the Nobel Peace Prize, having negotiated a cease-fire in the Middle East while serving as a United Nations diplomat.

And, in July 1950, Alice Marble, a top-ranked U.S. tennis player, would jolt the game's hierarchy by publicly condemning the USLTA for denying Althea Gibson the opportunity to compete at the U.S. National Championships. Marble's conscience-disturbing words would prompt the USLTA to accept Gibson's application, a decision in September 1950 that allowed her to become the first black to compete in the prestigious U.S. National Championships (U.S. Open since 1968).

THE CHARLOTTESVILLE CHALLENGE

Pushed by that steady breeze of change, Johnson saw no reason why Charlottesville, home of Virginia's first institute of higher education, should not also be persuaded to loosen its shackles on black folks. In the 1950s, the University of Virginia, like the rest of the South, clung to its 'separate, but equal' policy of racial segregation. But Johnson believed that an academic environment might be a good place to plant the seeds of racial revolution in the white world of high school tennis. He introduced himself to Edmund 'Teddy' Penzold, the referee of the Charlottesville interscholastic event, as Dr. Robert Walter Johnson, commissioner of tennis for the Negro high schools in Virginia. He knew his M.D. would get most men's attention, if not their respect.

He told Penzold that he had a tennis court at his home, where he trained young blacks to play and that his dream was to see young blacks play in this event. His desire, he said, was to bring about competitive change, not social. If allowed to play, he promised that his boys would not try to eat there, sleep there or use any of the other campus facilities. In essence, he'd get the boys to the courts, watch them play their matches, and then get out of town by sundown, maybe sooner.

Penzold latched on to Johnson's proposal. He told Johnson that if he could find any black juniors of outstanding caliber, he would consider letting them enter next year's event.

"Give me your address and I'll send you an application this winter," Penzold said.

Johnson, who confined his search to the Lynchburg area, selected Dunbar High School's Victor Miller and Roosevelt Megginson as his Charlottesville pioneers. In June 1951, they became the first blacks to compete in the national high school event, a noteworthy achievement. However, Johnson considered their performances feeble efforts, at best. "They were annihilated in the first round," Johnson said. "I was embarrassed."

Miller lost 6-0, 6-0 to Carl Norgoner, of Scarsborough Prep, New York. "I got the collar all right," Miller said. Johnson compared Miller's effort to that of a mule on a racetrack. Megginson played with comparable disgrace, losing 6-0, 6-0 to Al Harum of Coral Gables, Florida.

Johnson apologized to Penzold for his players' performances because he knew that they fell far short of the "outstanding caliber" that Penzold expected to see. More important, Johnson knew that Penzold's decision angered and caused concern among many of his white friends and neighbors.

Years later, William L. Clover, a Charlottesville businessman and the USLTA Interscholastic tournament director, would admit there was even thought of giving up the event if Penzold was going to continue aiding Johnson.

"There was a feeling expressed by one individual," Clover said, "that if this was the case, maybe we should let some other university handle it. And there were others who felt that way. Of course, it's hard to understand—at this distance—the feeling in those days."

However, Penzold's supporters included Dr. Colgate Darden, who was the university's president from 1947 to 1959. A World War I aviator and Virginia's governor from 1942 to 1946, Darden reorganized the state's civil defense, reformed its prisons and set up retirement plans for state employees and secondary school teachers.

"Colgate supported Teddy all the way," Penzold's wife, Lucy, said. "Teddy insisted that this thing be done fairly despite the complaints. He was very adamant that blacks be allowed to play. All he cared about was whether you played good tennis; that was the only basis."

As head of the Port Authority in Norfolk, Virginia, Penzold was a prominent figure in the Tidewater area. He loved tennis and, like Johnson, wanted to teach others how to play. He understood and appreciated what Johnson wanted to do. "He had a group of young people he tried to push into tennis," Clover said. "He coached them and sponsored them. They became known as the 'Teddy Bears.'"

After listening to Johnson mumble an apology regarding Miller and Megginson's effort, Penzold urged him to focus on developing a national event for the nation's most talented black junior players. "Expand your search for young Negro talent," he said. "Organize a Negro national interscholastic championship. Hold it in May and I assure you the finalists will be able to play in Charlottesville in June."

Buoyed by Penzold's promise, Johnson quickly established a plan of action. Though tennis was a rarity in black communities, he knew that the American Tennis Association (ATA), a predominantly black organization that was founded in 1916 by a group of black doctors, lawyers and businessmen, would provide some candidates. He formed a committee of friends and associates who belonged to ATA clubs throughout the country. He contacted Dr. John Wheeler and William Lionel Cook of Durham, North Carolina; Dr. Hubert Eaton of Wilmington, North Carolina; Dr. John McGriff, Jr. of Portsmouth, Virginia; William (Babes) Jones of Baltimore, Maryland; Arthur Chippey, of Orangeburg, South Carolina; Tom Harris of Richmond, Virginia; and E.L. McCauley of Raleigh, North Carolina.

Aided by this group, which later became known as the ATA's Junior Development Committee, Johnson created the black national interscholastic tennis championships, which began in May of 1952. Twenty-three players from 10 high schools participated in the inaugural event, held in 1952 at Virginia Union University in Richmond, Virginia. William Winn, a left-hander from Wilmington, North Carolina, and Elton King, a right-hander from Washington, D.C., were the finalists. Penzold kept his promise, allowing both players to compete in the USLTA Interscholastic Championships.

Neither Winn nor King won a match that year in Charlottesville, but both were competitive, especially Winn, who lost to Barry MacKay of Dayton, Ohio, 6-2, 6-1. "Billy Winn was one of the fastest boys ever to play on the junior team," Johnson wrote in the 1959 ATA National program. "He possessed good anticipation, learned quickly and was a very good competitor. It was a big loss to the tennis world when he quit tennis after receiving a four-year college scholarship."

With his junior development program in place, Johnson was confident that Winn would be replaced. Each year, the team of players he sent to Charlottesville grew larger and advanced further in the field. "My ambition was to develop someone who could win the USLTA Interscholastic Championship," he said. "That was it, pure and simple."

After a few years, instead of wanting his players to be competitive with the white players, Johnson saw the title as an achievable goal, despite what others were saying.

"What made me maddest," Johnson told the *Washington Post* in 1969, "was this idea that colored athletes were only good as sprinters or strong boys, (who) couldn't learn . . . finesse. And somewhere I read an article that said, flat out, there would never be a great Negro tennis player."

Even with Penzold's support, Johnson knew that there would be obstacles, especially for the more assertive players, who would strike back if attacked—verbally or physically. If they wouldn't accept the Jackie Robinson turn-the-other-cheek lifestyle in baseball, they wouldn't go to Charlottesville or to any of the other integrated events he planned to challenge.

At 52, Robert Walter Johnson already had seen and weathered the worst of the nation's deeply embedded hostilities toward blacks. Soft-spoken and self-assured, he moved through life with the air of an aristocrat. He believed he had the proper mixture of wisdom, wealth, determination and confidence to achieve what many considered an impossible dream. No doubt, he inherited his defy-all-odds mentality from his father, known affectionately by his friends and family in Plymouth, North Carolina, as Papa Jerry.

2

Family

Jerry Johnson met Nancy Scott in 1895 at a carnival just outside Plymouth, North Carolina, his hometown. Back then a carnival was a social love-fest, a come-one, come-all gathering of family and neighbors, mingling comfortably at a countywide picnic.

Farmers brought their best stock to compete for prizes. Children played tag in the fields. Young men and women mostly eyed each other from afar, but the bolder ones took strolls along paths leading into the woods. Peripatetic mothers unpacked picnic baskets, watched over the youngsters in the fields and, more than occasionally, looked toward the paths leading into the woods.

Jerry was 21; Nancy was 15. Though he felt love in the air, Jerry kept his distance, never made a romantic move toward Nancy, whom he learned was from nearby Williamston, North Carolina. He sneaked glances at her only when she looked the other way. Deep inside, he knew this epitome of loveliness soon would become his partner for life.

Jerry stood five feet six inches, had dark brown skin and the upper torso of a weightlifter. Nancy was about an inch shorter, with light brown skin and a dazzling head of long black hair.

Skin color was often a divisive factor among blacks, even long after slavery. At the turn of the 20th century, blacks of all shades still traveled on the unequal side of America's "separate but equal" roads of justice, but light-skinned blacks found the road less bumpy. Black children growing up in the segregated South often summarized the impact of the color line with this verse: "If you're black, stand back; if you're brown, hang around; if you're yellow, you're mellow; and if you're white, you're all right."

The difference in skin tone among blacks in the South began during slavery. For the most part, these light-skinned blacks were the illegitimate children of white plantation owners and their sons, many of whom kept female slaves as concubines. Some plantation owners used white females to work in their mansions. The fair-skinned slaves worked in the house and, generally, received better treatment than the slaves who worked the fields. Jerry was the son of a field worker; Nancy was the daughter of a house servant. More significantly, Nancy's grandmother was a white indentured slave. At the time, some whites were sold to plantation owners as indentured slaves, bound by a contractual agreement to work for their owners for a given length of time.

At the turn of the 19th century, an indentured white slave named Nancy Scott was the property of a plantation owner in a section of Williamston called Tyner Town. She had children sired by the son of the plantation owner and children sired by a black slave. In 1880, Mary Celia Scott, who was a daughter of the indentured slave Nancy Scott and a black slave, gave birth to Nancy, named after her grandmother.

Visions of Nancy rolled through Jerry's head long after the carnival was a distant memory. He went to his job at the lumber mill each day, lugging her image in his mind's eye.

Born and raised in Norfolk, Virginia, Jerry followed his employer, the John L. Roper Lumber Company, to a section of Washington County now called Roper. He worked for his uncle, Henry Trafton, who was a contractor for the lumber company, which was based in Richmond, Virginia.

In 1890, the company built a mill in a settlement called Lee's Mill. Settlers built homes and shelters from an endless supply of pine, cypress, oak, hickory, ash, gum and juniper. The Roper Company became one of the world's largest lumber operations and the economic boom that resulted inspired residents of Lee's Mill to change the town's name to Roper.

Like Jerry, scores of families from Virginia moved with the company to this rural North Carolina town to keep their jobs. Since the carnival, love, not money, had Jerry believing that he had made the right decision. As a member of Uncle Henry's crew, Jerry cut timber along the shores of the Roanoke River and loaded it onto barges and rafts. Afterward, he rode to Williamston on his bicycle and pedaled back and forth past Nancy's house, which was on a steep hill. One day, he was invited inside. And the courtship began.

Two years later, Jerry John Johnson married Nancy Scott at a Baptist church in Roper. They lived there for a year before the company transferred Jerry back to Norfolk. Nancy became pregnant during that first year, but the child was stillborn. She became pregnant again the following year, and on April 16, 1899, screams from a baby boy brought sighs of relief and tears of joy to the beaming faces of his nervous parents. The timing of Robert Walter Johnson's birth was especially satisfying to Jerry. His first son came into this world on the same day Papa Jerry had been born 25 years earlier. Father and son shared many choruses of "Happy Birthday" together.

Papa Jerry was a quick study in nearly everything he did. His formal school training was limited to graduation from Norfolk Mission College, which provided, at the time, the equivalence of an elementary education. He could read and write and was a wizard at arithmetic.

Thanks to years of guidance from Uncle Henry, Papa Jerry became an astute businessman, as well as a skilled logger. Papa Jerry loved a challenge. Most contractors avoided any job that required cutting a plot of land in the swamps or in heavy rain. Papa Jerry never did. He took logging jobs no other contractor would touch and always figured out ways to get that job done, while making a profit.

Papa Jerry became the company's fair-headed boy, though there was nothing fair about his head or skin. His efficiency and drive opened the doors to status and financial advancement beyond his dreams. The John Roper Lumber Company transferred Papa Jerry and his family—at company expense—back to Plymouth. The company also gave him a home, a comfortable white cottage at 216 Adams St. Before his family moved in, the house, located in a white neighborhood, was painted and renovations were made to Papa Jerry's specifications. Neighbors assumed another white family was moving in.

No one complained when the Johnson family of five showed up. Two daughters, Victoria and Eva, joined the family before they moved to Plymouth. A baby brother, Roy, arrived shortly after they had settled into their new home. A few years later, Papa Jerry built a playhouse for Roy in the backyard near the chicken coop. It was an ideal place for little Robert and his sister, Victoria, to play their favorite game.

"We used to go out in that playhouse just about every day and play doctor and nurse," Victoria said. "He was the doctor; I was the nurse. After mama would leave the house, we used to catch a few of the biddies—you know, baby chickens—make a little bed of hay for them, tie their wings and tie their feet. Then Robert, who was 10 at the time, would go outside and come back wearing specs and carrying a black satchel. I don't know where he got the satchel or specs. He would ask me, 'How's the patient?' Then he would examine the patients.

"Sometimes he would prescribe castor oil for the patients. So I'd give the chicks castor oil. Sometimes he would prescribe salt. So I'd give them salt. It went like that all day 'til mama would come home. Mama would look at the biddies, see how drugged they looked and say, 'What happened to the chickens?' And we'd say we didn't know. Robert always used to talk about being a doctor when he grew up. That's why he used to practice on those chickens."

When he was 15, Robert worked at the Plymouth Box and Panel Company. He earned 65 cents a day, making boxes and panels. At 18, he went to Virginia Beach for the summer and worked as a waiter. However, Papa Jerry, who became one of Plymouth's most prominent businessmen, provided Robert with most of his work experience during his teenage years. At one point, Papa Jerry owned a furniture store, a grocery store, an auditorium where dances and movies were shown and other properties.

"Colored folks and white folks used to stop at my father's stores," Victoria said. "White folks always treated my father with respect. Several times, he had to go to court to sue people who owed him, and he never lost a case. Never.

"He had good, common sense. You couldn't fool him. He was a hustler and nobody could beat him counting money. He broke a pool stick over a man's head for calling him a liar. From that day on, nobody ever called him a liar."

Quite simply, Papa Jerry was a tough businessman and a great logger. People in the lumber business knew this well. Most of Papa Jerry's income was derived from his work as a logging contractor, and he often times had up to 30 men on his payroll. The lumber company paid him a fee for clearing a specific plot of land and transporting the logs by barge to the mill. Papa Jerry supervised the job and paid his workers afterward. The loggers were paid out of a suitcase full of money that Papa Jerry carried with him. Whatever was left belonged to Papa Jerry.

Papa Jerry trained young Robert to be his accountant. Robert wrote receipts, recorded personal data, and kept travel and other related business expenses. Papa Jerry also sponsored a semi-pro baseball team and Robert kept records and statistics for it, too. Robert became as adept as his dad at handling funds. Papa Jerry's oldest son was developing other interests, too.

He was two inches taller than his father and, when shirtless, exposed a similar well-developed physique. Easy to smile, Robert was handsome brown. He often brought color to a young woman's cheeks with his seductive eyes. Victoria thought of him as a ladies man in training. If he couldn't charm the young lasses with his good looks, he'd reel them in with smooth lines and expensive taste.

"He used to make Eva and me go out and pick May peas and sell them," Victoria said, "so he could take his girlfriend to the silent screen show. Used to make me so mad because we'd go to the show and he'd be sitting up in the reserved seats with his girlfriend and we'd be sitting in back on the benches. We'd do it though because if we didn't, he'd tell mama about our boyfriends."

The Johnson family endured a great deal of stress and many embarrassing moments due to Robert's Romeo ways. When Robert was 17, a young girl who became pregnant said Robert was the child's father. Robert questioned the girl's claim, saying the girl had slept with other boys as well. Despite Robert's denials, Papa Jerry and Mama Nancy agreed to help support the baby girl.

Robert spent most of his teen years chasing his other passion: football. He graduated from Plymouth Elementary School and attended high school at Elizabeth City State Normal School in Elizabeth City, North Carolina. He got his first taste of organized football there and couldn't wait for more. He was a strong tackler and a fast runner.

WHIRLWIND

By 1915, Papa Jerry and Mama Nancy were raising six youngsters: Robert, Victoria, Eva, Roy, Ruth Olivia and one-year-old Samuel DeLeon. Having six mouths to feed didn't prevent the family from enjoying the luxuries of that time. In fact, they were the first black family in Plymouth to have indoor toilets and electricity, the first to own a radio and the first to own an automobile.

"Papa Jerry was a good provider," his daughter Eva said.

Papa Jerry had no illusions about the dangers associated with the white South's attitude toward people of color. He understood clearly that white men were the only free men in America. Papa Jerry was a year old when Congress passed the Civil Rights Bill of 1875, prohibiting discrimination in such public accommodations as hotels, theaters and amusement parks. Eight years later, the Supreme Court declared that law unconstitutional.

In 1890, the Mississippi constitutional convention began the systematic exclusion of Negroes from the political arena by adopting a battery of complex tests as prerequisites to voting. Seven other states, including North Carolina, had followed suit by 1910. The great racial divide was established firmly in 1896 when the Supreme Court, in the Plessy vs. Ferguson case, upheld the doctrine of "separate but equal," thus paving the way for the segregation of Negroes throughout the South.

A revival of the Ku Klux Klan began in Alabama and spread all the way to California. Membership in the KKK, one of the nation's first terrorist organizations, reached four million in 1920, the year Robert turned 21. That year, Papa Jerry and other Negroes in Plymouth got an up close and personal glimpse of KKK-style racism.

A band of Klansmen, dressed in white robes, made a late-night stop at a country store owned by Rob Taylor, a light-skinned black. Victoria believed the Klan targeted Taylor for "tipping his hat or winking at a white woman." Someone else said they got him because he cursed at a white man. Didn't matter. Klan-inspired fear swirled through Plymouth's black population.

The Klansmen took Rob Taylor to a field, tied him to a tree and used acid to burn the letter 'K' on his forehead and on both cheeks. Papa Jerry and some friends cut Taylor loose and took him to a doctor in another town. A few days later, the Klan returned and threatened to do the same to Papa Jerry.

"Just don't bother my wife; just get me," Papa Jerry said.

Young Robert was attending classes at Shaw University in Raleigh, North Carolina, during the Klan visit. When Robert learned of the threat to his father, he found reasons to visit home more often.

3

Out of Control

At Shaw University, Robert got to do what he loved best: play sports and play around with pretty young women. He proved to be a past master at both. Robert couldn't confine himself to one sport anymore than he could confine his attention to one woman.

Few could match his smooth swing of a baseball bat or his ball-handling abilities on a basketball court. Football, however, was his first love, and with his quickness and daring jaunts on the gridiron, Robert established himself as the rising star at Shaw.

To Robert's delight, pretty young coeds, even in 1919, were drawn to the campus' super jocks. Robert's exploits on the football field brought several women rushing into his social life, but none quickened the beat of his heart as much as Annie Pate, a 16-year-old high school student from Goldsboro, North Carolina. She had "good hair and nice color," which among blacks in those days meant she had smooth straight hair and light skin.

Annie had no intentions of letting skin color interfere with her chance of getting to know Robert, the football hunk. Annie, who attended high school classes on Shaw's campus, was flattered that a handsome college boy wanted to help her understand the game's nuances. Robert's status as a big man on campus overshadowed his dark brown skin. Annie attended every game and, with Robert's help, learned to appreciate and understand the fundamentals. Robert told her what team members talked about while huddling before each play. He tried to persuade her to do a little one-on-one huddling after the games, but Annie stiff-armed those attempts.

"She was very nice-looking and a very nice girl," said Clifton Jones, a fellow-student at Shaw when Robert and Annie were there. "Robert was trying to go with her and trying to make her do things she didn't want to do. Everybody at Shaw used to go on this picnic every spring. He was with Annie and he tried to take advantage of her, but she wouldn't let him. She told him, 'Tennessee, you may see, but under this dress you'll never be.'"

Papa Jerry and Mama Nancy didn't raise Robert to be the kind of man who'd force himself on a woman. Throughout his childhood, Robert responded unhesitatingly to the rules of life set down by Papa Jerry and Mama Nancy, who were strict disciplinarians. The girls in the family did the housework and helped take care of the garden; the boys cut wood, cleaned the yard and all other outdoor chores. No one went anywhere or joined any organization without parental permission. Sometimes when Robert left Shaw to return to Plymouth for summer vacation and holidays, he had to be reminded that at home there still were rules to be followed, respect to be shown.

"One time he thought he was going to go out to a dance without asking permission," his sister Eva said. "All day, he kept asking mama how she liked his coat or tie with the shirt he was going to wear to the dance, but he never asked her permission to go. So when he was getting ready to go out the door, mama asked him where he thought he was going. He said, 'Mama, you know I've been talking about going to the dance all day.' She said, 'Yes, but you never asked permission to go. So you get right upstairs, take those clothes off and go to bed.' And that's what he did.

"Sister (Victoria) and I went to mama and pleaded with her to let him go to the dance, but she wouldn't change her mind. Later, she said, 'I didn't let Robert go to the dance because I didn't want him to think he could ever disobey his parents, no matter how old he was.'"

With no parents to guide him, Robert established his own rules to follow at Shaw. His main rule, it seemed, was that there would be no rules to keep him from chasing women. For the pleasure of spending private time with pretty coeds, he routinely took risks and broke rules. Disobedience led to his dismissal in his sophomore year when he and two other male students were caught overnight in the girls' dormitory. That was an absolute no-no at the small Baptist university, founded in 1865 by Dr. Henry M. Tupper, a young minister from Massachusetts.

Despite his brilliance on the football field, Robert Walter Johnson wouldn't leave Shaw with a degree. Shaw administrators didn't expel Robert, but in the spring of 1921, they urged him to make arrangements to continue his college education elsewhere.

Young blacks eager to be educated had little trouble gaining entry to any of the black colleges during that time. Robert's next stop was Virginia Union University, which also was a church-affiliated institution. No women attended Virginia Union and no gambling was allowed. Once again, Robert chose to ignore the rules by hosting poker parties in his dormitory room. He was expelled within a school year.

With two strikes against him, Robert, then 21, bumped into trouble at every turn. Friends and relatives told him that he was out of control and that he needed to calm down, to end his wild ways. Some suggested marriage as a possible stabilizer. Despite all his woes, Robert continued to date Annie Pate. She accepted his love and friendship, but maintained her "no sex" policy. During one summer visit to the Pate's family home in Goldsboro, Robert asked Annie's mother to allow him to take Annie to Plymouth to meet his family.

Mother Pate wasn't about to let her daughter travel with Plymouth's most notorious wolf, at least not before neutralizing the wolf trap. "Annie can go to Plymouth with you, Robert, but only as Mrs. Robert Walter Johnson." Shortly afterward, they were married at a Methodist church in Goldsboro. The Reverend James C. Taylor, who would re-enter their lives later, presided. Robert's family members didn't attend because Robert didn't let them know about it. He decided to spring Annie on them as a surprise, and he couldn't imagine them disapproving of his lovely new bride. However, when Robert and Annie arrived in Plymouth, they discovered that Robert wasn't the first of Mama Nancy's children to tie the knot without parental approval.

His sister, Victoria, had beaten him to the punch. Papa Jerry met

Robert and Annie at the front door, and before Robert could say a decent hello and make his dramatic announcement, Papa Jerry gave him a believe-it-or-not news flash:

"You're not going to believe this, Robert, but Sister (Victoria) has gone off and married Alex Bonds. Didn't tell anybody, didn't ask permission. She just eloped. What you got to say to that?"

Clearly, Papa Jerry wasn't in the frame of mind to deal with a similar news flash from his eldest son. So Robert, showing a mind as quick as his feet, went to "Plan B" and introduced Annie as a girlfriend. Annie shared a room with Robert's sisters during her brief stay. She told them of their marriage. They kept it a secret. Robert's sisters called Annie, "Sister Pate," and made her feel at home.

Mama Nancy learned of the marriage about a week later when she received a letter from Annie's mother. Even Mama Nancy agreed that Victoria's marriage to Alex Bonds was all the excitement that Papa Jerry could handle for one summer. So they waited a few months before telling him about Robert getting hitched.

The marriage helped Robert reach a level of maturity that he never knew as a bachelor. With Annie to care for, he developed a greater sense of determination, commitment and responsibility. He had been forced to leave two colleges because of poor judgment. In his gut, he knew his third shot at receiving a sheepskin would be his last.

The Klan's visit to Plymouth put a scare in Robert and he knew that despite his father's success as a businessman, life would never be easy for black folks in the South. (He was 16 at the time of the "Great Migration," during which more than two million Southern blacks moved to industrial cities in the North.) Two years later, he read about more than 10,000 blacks marching down Fifth Avenue in New York City to protest the lynching of blacks in the South. He decided that a move north might put him on the right track.

Two of Robert's instructors at Shaw had graduated from a black college near Philadelphia, Pennsylvania. Robert remembered that they talked often about Lincoln University's football program, its brilliant white teachers and about graduates who later became physicians after leaving Lincoln. He decided that Lincoln was where he wanted to be.

Annie helped Robert pack and prepare to resume college life at Lincoln. He left for Lincoln with a different marital status and mindset; she left for Goldsboro with the hope in her heart that Robert would be strong and true. She believed that Robert would follow his dream of becoming a physician. Still, she knew that his passion for football could very well become a major stumbling block.

4

Whirlwind

IN THE EARLY 1920S, while Knute Rockne was turning Notre Dame, a small Catholic university in South Bend, Indiana, into a college football power, the legend of "Whirlwind" sprouted at Lincoln, a small black university near Oxford, Pennsylvania.

Kicked out of Shaw and Virginia Union, Robert faced a third strike far away from family and friends, in a place where nobody knew his name. He arrived on campus in time for football practice in the summer of 1922, eager to capture a spot on the starting team, destined to leave an unmatched legacy as a running back.

Before Robert arrived, Lincoln already had established itself as the nation's black college football power. In 1921, Lincoln's roster included a couple of behemoth linesmen of that time: L.L. "Battleship" Carter, who was five feet eleven inches tall and weighed 211 pounds, and C.L. "Big Boy" Morgan, who was five feet eleven inches tall and weighed 198 pounds. The Lincoln Lions finished the 1921 season with a 4-1 record. They beat Bordentown 26-0, Morgan State 33-0, Hampton Institute 13-0 and Howard University 13-7. The Lions' dominance of the Colored Intercollegiate Athletic Association (later changed to the Central Intercollegiate Athletic Association) was spoiled by a 1-0 forfeit to Virginia Union.

A bit older and more seasoned than his teammates, Robert was smooth and shifty in practice sessions. Still, as a rookie and an outsider, he knew it was far more important to earn his teammates' respect on the gridiron at game-time, not on the practice field. At Shaw and Virginia

Union, Robert was an exceptional running back, but showed brilliance as a hardnosed defensive player. At Lincoln, he raised his offensive game to new heights.

Lincoln beat Bordentown 9-0 in the season opener and spanked Harrisburg 34-0 the following week, with Robert scoring two touchdowns. Lincoln faced Morgan State in the third game and that's when Robert, who refused to wear a helmet, ran wild. He dipped, dodged and stutter-stepped his way to a university record eight touchdowns, leading Lincoln to a 56-0 battering of the Morgan State Bears. Robert went to classes the following week as an overnight hero, with his teammates among his chief admirers.

Said Hildrus A. Poindexter, the right guard on Lincoln's offensive line who helped create the holes that led to Robert's break-loose gallops in that game and others, "Johnson used to get in the huddle and look at me and say, 'Poindexter, we need five yards. Can you give it to us?' And I'd say 'Johnson, we're going to get you that five yards.' And that was all he needed. Not only could he run fast, he was good at sidestepping, stiff-arming and breaking tackles. I don't know anyone who could stand on an opposing line and break through like he did. Johnson would get through and make his five yards and more."

Word traveled fast about the wondrous moves Robert was making on the football field. Indeed, when Lincoln visited Charleston, West Virginia, to play West Virginia State University, more than 10,000 people—all anxious to catch a glimpse of Lincoln's unstoppable running back—packed the stadium. Even Ephraim Franklin Morgan, the state's governor showed up, along with Houston G. Young, Morgan's secretary of state, and Charleston Mayor Grant P. Hall.

West Virginia wasted little time making Robert feel unwelcome. The home team's defense battered Robert in the first quarter, repeatedly knocking him to the ground with punishing tackles. Robert left the game limping before the first half ended, with West Virginia leading 19-0. The second half began with Robert still on the sidelines, nursing a leg injury, but he trotted along the sidelines near the end of the third quarter, testing his leg. When the fourth quarter began, Robert, with fire-in-the-belly determination and a stirring presence, led the Lions on a touchdown drive.

WHIRLWIND

"He struck the pose of a typical figure of an ancient leader," Poindexter said, describing Robert's impact on his teammates when they were in the huddle and helping him streak down the field on a long run. "Wearing a helmet was optional. He had let his hair grow long, slicked it back and wouldn't wear a helmet. And there he'd go running down the field with his hair flowing back, streaking and looking like a whirlwind. I guess that's why they started calling him that."

Said George D. Cannon, who, as the Lincoln trainer that year, had a sideline view of Whirlwind's unforgettable performance against West Virginia, "He got out there and his hair was flying all around and he was stutter-stepping through the line. Must have gotten loose for long gains about five times."

Whirlwind led the Lions on a second touchdown drive, but time ran out before the Lions could muster another. West Virginia defeated Lincoln 19-14, but Whirlwind more than satisfied the curiosity of the fans that had flocked to see him. They left in a buzz, spreading the news about the running back that had burst through holes like a whirling dervish, claiming the nickname that would stay with him for the rest of his life.

"He was the sensation of the game," Cannon said. "The papers, the people in the town, everybody talked about how he was dashing through the line like a whirlwind."

The next day, a West Virginia sports reporter described Johnson's performance this way: "With Whirlwind Johnson tearing gaping holes in the yellow sweatered line of the Institute eleven, the Lincoln University team staged a comeback in the final quarter of their clash with Institute yesterday afternoon that threatened to overcome the 19-point lead of the West Virginians."

Another reporter wrote: "With hair standing straight up, that warrior of the gridiron ploughed his way through the line of the opposition time after time for substantial gains. With the ball on the five-yard line twice it was his plunging that took it over for the points that threatened the lead of the Institute."

Hampton Institute edged Lincoln 9-7 the following week, and then the Lions turned it around, winning their last three games. They beat Wilberforce 13-12, St. Paul 18-0 and Howard 13-12, finishing with a 6-2 record and a season stuffed full of memories of Whirlwind, a CIAA gridiron legend.

The nickname seemed appropriate for Robert on or off the football field. He joined Lincoln's baseball team, debating team, Omega Psi Phi fraternity and the Black Hand Club, which, through its motto, encouraged its members to "Do it with song and let that song be jazz." Qualifications for membership? "Good jokes, musical inclination and expert dancing ability."

Whirlwind also organized and coached a basketball team for the Omegas that supposedly was stronger than the school's varsity team. He seemed everywhere at once. And with Annie in Goldsboro, Whirlwind found time to share his tales of the gridiron with women eager to be seen with Lincoln's elusive legendary running back. On one occasion, he used his way with women to help Poindexter find a meaningful social life.

"Whirlwind knew a lot of women," Poindexter said. "Once he said, 'Poindexter, I'm going to get you a girl!' So one day he introduced me to the woman who became my wife. He was very urbane, had good manners and could talk to anybody. And people enjoyed talking to him. Girls enjoyed dancing with him and men enjoyed his company because he was all man, very masculine."

While Whirlwind was helping Poindexter find romance, Poindexter helped Whirlwind settle down in a different manner. At night, Whirlwind often relied on Poindexter, whom he dubbed "the bookworm," to help him keep his eyes in his books, instead of on his latest comely admirer.

"He was having some trouble with inorganic chemistry one semester; so I helped him through that," Poindexter said.

Poindexter was as much a gifted superstar in the classroom as he was on the football field. After graduating from Lincoln, he spent two years at Dartmouth before working toward a medical degree from Harvard, which he received in 1929. He received an A.B. degree in microbiology from Columbia University in 1930 and a Ph.D. in microbiology and immunology from Columbia in 1932. Poindexter became one of the world's foremost scientists in tropical diseases. As a commissioned officer during World War II, he often made life-saving decisions regarding the location of Allied soldiers fighting in the jungles of the South Pacific.

Despite Whirlwind's various extracurricular activities, including a rather heavy social calendar, he rarely neglected his assignments. Like many of Lincoln's students, he was committed to his studies and often spent weekends and holidays on campus, getting extra help from an unusually dedicated cadre of college professors. High purpose and commitment were the norm at this extraordinary institution of higher learning, which was founded in 1854, nearly 11 years before the Civil War ended.

It was called Ashmun Institute in its early years and received its current name shortly after the assassination of President Abraham Lincoln in 1865. Founder John Miller Dickey's primary goals were "to educate Negro ministers for the evangelization of Africa and to provide for the religious leadership of Negro people in the U.S."

In 1866, the curriculum included schools of law, medicine and theology, but the schools of law and medicine were closed in 1873. Located in eastern Pennsylvania, about 50 miles west of Philadelphia, Lincoln was an all-male college. The students rarely ventured into Oxford, the nearest city, because it was segregated.

"A few of the guys from the South would go to the movies and sit in the colored seats, but if you were from the North, that kind of thing burned you up," said Cannon, a New Yorker.

"And if we got in trouble in the city, we'd be in trouble at Lincoln, too," Poindexter said. "They understood our feelings, but their position was Lincoln men don't cause trouble."

In the early '20s, Lincoln's faculty consisted primarily of graduates of the Princeton Seminary College.

"I'd say the faculty was about 90 percent Princeton graduates," Poindexter said. "None of them was concerned about how much money they made. They were doing missionary work. They were truly the most dedicated people I had ever seen. They were men who respected God, men of integrity."

They were men who stood ready and eager to help their students at any time, in their respective areas of expertise. Professor Walter

Livingston Wright helped those who struggled with mathematics. Professor Arthur James offered assistance in chemistry. English professors William Finney and Richard Hill often gave up their weekends to help students enjoy the works of great writers, including Shakespeare.

"I was having trouble with 'The Merchant of Venice,'" Poindexter said. "Professor Finney said, 'What you're doing is just saying words; now go back and read.'"

But Lincoln's most respected teacher at the time was professor Harold Grim, a light-haired, bespectacled graduate of Leigh University who taught biology.

"We dissected the cat, the salamander, the grasshopper, and just about everything else," George Cannon said. "Grim taught us how. He taught everything in the biological sciences. He taught bacteriology, which most other colleges didn't offer at the undergraduate level. When I left Lincoln and went to the University of Chicago to study medicine, they told me they were quite sure that I would have to take an undergraduate course in bacteriology because, usually, nobody had had bacteriology. I said, 'Oh yes, I had bacteriology!' So they looked at my record and there it was.

"Harvard didn't even give bacteriology in undergraduate school. And Harvard guys in my class couldn't understand that a little Negro school that they had never heard of offered a course that they didn't get. I didn't have to take the course and the guys from Harvard did. So I was very proud of Lincoln at the time and very proud of Grim."

Poindexter experienced a similar reaction when he went to Dartmouth after graduating from Lincoln. "One of the professors examined my bacteriology notes and said, 'This is as good as we give here at Dartmouth.'"

Many of the Lincoln professors held doctor of philosophy degrees, but Grim had only a master's.

"But he was a teacher," Cannon said. "To show you how he taught so you'd never forget, we were studying the germ that causes gonorrhea and one of the students asked, 'Professor Grim, can you catch gonorrhea off a toilet seat?' His answer was 'That would be a terrible place to take a woman.' Here I am 60 years later, quoting him word for word. Now, that's a teacher. He preached a lot too. In fact, he was always talking about the body that God gave you. 'Take care of it. Preserve it.' "

Whirlwind rarely followed Grim's edict for bodily preservation when he played football. He was a fearless runner, a player who'd take nearly any risk to lead his team to victory. His teammates rewarded his fearlessness by selecting him captain of the 1923 squad. The Lions opened the season with a 7-0 victory against West Virginia, but lost to Hampton 7-3 the following week. They tied St. Paul 3-3 and then thrashed Shaw 48-0. Whirlwind had a field day against the North Carolina Baptist college that two years earlier had sent him packing. One newspaper account of the game read: "Whirlwind Johnson, Lincoln's fullback and captain, was the star. Johnson was a terror at end runs, line plunges and everything else to be done. He passed and received passes, tackled like a fiend and ran back punts in a manner that was a pleasure to behold. He scored most of the touchdowns."

Whirlwind ended his collegiate football career at Lincoln on Thanksgiving Day in 1923 in Philadelphia's National League Park. More than 27,000 fans watched Lincoln defeat Howard University 47-0. Later, Whirlwind and Poindexter were named to the Negro All-American team.

Whirlwind and Poindexter were among a special breed of high achievers who attended Lincoln that year. Of the 54 graduates in the 1924 class, 25 percent continued their education at various medical schools and became physicians. At the time, Lincoln was producing 10 percent of the black physicians in the United States.

Whirlwind, No. 38 of 54 graduates, finished Lincoln with a 2.9 grade point average on a 4.0 scale. Lincoln had prepared him for his next step: medical school. But Whirlwind wasn't quite ready for the even greater mental grind that goes with striving to be a medical doctor. He chose instead to hold on awhile longer to his Whirlwind persona. He left Lincoln to coach football, believing that he might at least pass on to others the knowledge and spirit that had helped him become Whirlwind.

5

A Coaching Phase

WHEN HE RETURNED to the family home in Roper in the spring of 1924, Robert received a hero's welcome—and not just because of his exploits as Whirlwind. As the first family member to graduate from college, he'd set an educational standard of excellence that each of his brothers and sisters would strive to equal. Papa Jerry and Mama Nancy's brood had become as large as the football squad Whirlwind had led at Lincoln.

In pecking order following Whirlwind, there was Victoria, Eva, Roy, Ruth Olivia, Samuel DeLeon, Eileen Eldorado, Elaine and Rupert. Big families were the norm in those days. Mama Nancy carried a babyload in her belly during 16 of 27 years of marriage. Jerry Jr. lived for only a week. Another infant, who had not been named, died two days after birth. The others died of assorted childhood diseases. Prenatal care was a yet-to-be-formed phrase in the field of medicine, and the infant mortality rate was one of many undocumented health tragedies in the black community. Only nine of Papa Jerry and Mama Nancy's children grew to adulthood. All became productive members of their respective communities. Here's a list of the siblings with their respective occupations:

Whirlwind, medical doctor;
Victoria, housewife;
Eva, elementary school principal;
Roy, chef;

A COACHING PHASE

Ruth Olivia, school teacher;
Samuel DeLeon, logger;
Eileen Eldorado, medical doctor;
Elaine, social worker; and
Rupert, high school coach.

Football and school work had kept Whirlwind at Lincoln during most holidays, so Annie rarely saw him. She had spent the two years attending North Carolina Teachers' College. She looked forward to sharing her bed with her husband on a daily basis. Whirlwind had spent the summer of 1923 in New York working as a redcap in Grand Central Station. His college degree gave him the edge he needed to become a Pullman porter, considered a prize job with the railroad company.

The Pullman Company, which at the time was among the most powerful business organizations in the nation, and the U.S. Post Office provided the best jobs for blacks in the 1920s. Pullman employed more blacks than any other company in the country, but only white men could be conductors. For the most part, the Pullman porters were house servants to the wealthy whites who rode in cars that were considered "hotels on wheels." The porters knew that they would have to, among other things, humor the passengers by providing "miles of smiles" during their work day. They also carried baggage, served food and shined shoes. The mostly white passengers entrusted their children to the care of the porters, who were available night and day.

Pullman porters earned $57 a month in 1925, but generous tips helped them make a decent living. The best porters—many of whom were college graduates—were intelligent and refined. They often worked in teams. If a porter had more shoes to shine than he could handle, a teammate would lend a hand.

However, Pullman porters often were cast as simpletons and/or clowns in the emerging entertainment media. In the early years of Hollywood, blacks portraying porters frequently were cast as buffoons, the butt of jokes or talking toys to amuse white children. Many porters lost their jobs by not accepting their Hollywood image. Some were dismissed for not looking happy, not smiling enough or not shining shoes to a passenger's satisfaction. Job security was nonexistent.

Working conditions began to improve in 1925 after Asa Philip Randolph launched a movement to provide higher wages and a better working environment for railroad workers. Twelve years later, the Pullman Company signed a contract with the Brotherhood of Sleeping Car Porters that paid union members $2 million and guaranteed them overtime pay. The deal established Randolph, a polished orator, as a significant civil rights activist of the '20s.

Annie didn't see much of Whirlwind that summer mainly because he spent most of it riding the trains along the eastern seaboard. And to her surprise, football continued to be a priority in her husband's life. Whirlwind and other former college football stars who worked as porters or redcaps spent some of their spare time in foot races in the train yards or dreaming of testing their skills against the likes of Jim Thorpe. A Native American born in Prague, Oklahoma, Thorpe won gold medals in the pentathlon and decathlon events in the 1912 Olympics and became the nation's first superstar football player. An All-American halfback as a collegian, Thorpe led the pre-NFL Canton Bulldogs to unofficial world championships in 1916-17 and 1919. He retired in 1928. Selected by the media as the most outstanding athlete of the first half of the 20th century, Thorpe, in 1920, became the first president of the American Professional Football Association.

Superstars of the CIAA rarely received national publicity, so the legend of Whirlwind lived primarily in black communities. Whirlwind was a rare jewel that never reached the white public's eye. In the fall of 1924, Robert took his extraordinary talents to Virginia Seminary College in Lynchburg, Virginia, where he began a career as a rookie coach. Eddie Hurt, a Howard University graduate who later built a football dynasty of his own at Morgan State University, assisted Robert.

"We won more games than we lost when Whirlwind was coaching," Hurt said. "But I don't remember exactly what our won-lost record was that year. Whirlwind was such a great athlete. We held scrimmages just about every day. He'd demonstrate everything. Then he'd take the ball in scrimmages to see if they could tackle him and most of the time, they couldn't.

"He would get on the side with the second team and reserves and

A COACHING PHASE

play against our starting varsity. Whirlwind and the reserves would beat the starting team in every practice. He was just that good."

Whirlwind coached football, basketball and baseball. Each team was nicknamed "the Whirlwinds." His exploits in football scrimmages received more attention than his team's efforts in games. Despite his successful coaching debut, Virginia Seminary College, then one of the CIAA's poorest institutions, couldn't offer him much more than lots of thanks. College President R.C. Woods paid the coaches out of his own pocket.

The school year ended with Whirlwind convinced that he could make a better living and gain far more recognition with another program. He returned to New York for a second summer of work as a Pullman porter, determined to find another college president who would be honored to have Whirlwind directing his athletic programs. He succeeded.

Each summer, New York's Grand Central Station became a convention center for the nation's most gifted athletes. When not working as redcaps or porters, they engaged in various forms of competition and exchanged information about life and conditions on their respective campuses. During a break from his redcap chores, Eddie Hurt learned that Morgan State was looking for coach and later moved to Baltimore. Robert found the coaching opportunity he wanted in Texas. Sam Houston College asked the swirling dervish to raise dust out west. Whirlwind was happy to oblige.

Whirlwind spent the 1925-26 school year coaching the Sam Houston "Whirlwinds" in football, basketball and baseball. Each team ended the year with a winning record.

On a personal level, Robert proved to be productive in the bedroom as well. Whirlwind went home for Christmas that year, and during that time, Robert Walter Jr., his only son, was conceived. Before Robert Jr. was born on September 5, 1926, Whirlwind already had moved to Atlanta, Georgia. Morris Brown College made him an offer he chose not to refuse. The pattern was unchanged. Whirlwind coached football, basketball and baseball. Each team had a winning season and each team was called the Morris Brown Whirlwinds.

WHIRLWIND

Whirlwind's appetite for women grew stronger in the Peach State. Even when Annie was with him, Whirlwind always seemed to have another woman on the sidelines of his social life. Annie never complained and Whirlwind never pretended to have eyes only for Annie.

Once, a woman friend from New York made Whirlwind a shirt that didn't have buttons. She told him to take it home and have his wife sew the buttons on, and that's what he did. One of Whirlwind's sisters told Annie not to sew buttons on a shirt that was given to him by another woman. But Annie claimed she didn't mind. She said it made more sense to put buttons on a homemade shirt, regardless of who made it, than to buy a new shirt. Times were too hard to be jealous about something like that, she rationalized.

The first sign that Annie's Atlanta fantasy world would come tumbling down occurred when Whirlwind met Hallie. Nicknamed Peggy, Hallie English was the secretary in the office of the president of Morris Brown College. She was light brown, shy and assuming. Whirlwind couldn't stay away from Peggy.

Whirlwind, Annie and Robert Jr. lived in a small white cottage on Mason Turner Avenue in Atlanta. Annie, who became ill after giving birth to Robert Jr., became a homebody. But even when she did go out for rides, Whirlwind invited Peggy to go with them. Whirlwind sat behind the wheel, Peggy sat next to Whirlwind and Annie, who sat by the passenger's window, never complained.

Whirlwind stayed at Morris Brown for a year, then accepted a coaching job with Atlanta University. O.G. Walker, a classmate of Whirlwind's at Lincoln, took Whirlwind's job at Morris Brown. Walker and his wife, Carrie, stayed with the Johnsons during their first year in Atlanta. Neither wife worked. Carrie cared for Annie, who was still in bad health, and Robert Jr., who was a year old. Still, the families struggled to make ends meet.

"Sometimes Whirlwind would help out by winning at poker," Carrie said. "That helped put some neck bones on the table. He was a hustler."

Whirlwind realized that coaching football was as close as he'd ever get to an ideal career in athletics. He found satisfaction in helping others strive for greatness on the gridiron, but not fulfillment. In the fall of 1928, Whirlwind shoved aside the joys of athletics to pursue a more challenging and aesthetic career. With savings from his summers working as a Pullman porter, combined with help from Papa Jerry, Whirlwind entered Meharry Medical College in Nashville, Tennessee.

    Annie prayed that she and Robert Jr. would go to Nashville with Whirlwind, but he decided otherwise. Too expensive for three, he said, and too great a potential to be distracted from his studies. Annie accepted his decision reluctantly. She had sensed a disturbance in their marriage since they had arrived in Atlanta. She knew the source of her uneasiness, but preferred to ignore it. She and Whirlwind had settled in Plymouth, North Carolina, when Whirlwind left for medical school. She hoped that this would be just another bump on the road. But deep inside, she feared that this time Whirlwind might do something that would turn this separation into a permanent arrangement.

6

A New Wife

THE STACK OF LETTERS was tucked in a corner of a suitcase that Whirlwind had sent to his parent's home in Plymouth. Annie decided to take a peek.

In her heart, she had known for more than a year that Whirlwind and Peggy were more than friends. It is one thing to wonder and suspect, quite another to stare down the barrel of a smoking gun. Page by painful page, Annie read the details of her husband's affair. Each line caused her to wince; each paragraph spiked her pulse rate. Though her eyes were full of tears, Annie finally could see clearly: The letters were, in essence, an obituary for their marriage.

Annie no longer had to read between the lines to know that Whirlwind had lied to her since the day he left for Nashville. While telling Annie that it would be too expensive for her to be with him at medical school, Whirlwind had made arrangements for Peggy to join him. They had lived there together for four years. Once Annie confronted him with the letters, Whirlwind asked her in every way he knew to end the marriage. Divorce in those days was akin to volunteering to spend the weekend with Satan. Depressed and feeling abandoned, Annie saw no other solution.

Whirlwind's older sisters, Victoria and Eva, felt Annie's pain. They loved her and tried their best to console her. Eva, who was a principal of an elementary school, got Annie a job as a teacher's aide in Smithfield, North Carolina. It wasn't much but it kept her mind off her plight, Eva reasoned. One day, Annie stopped by Eva's home and announced proudly that she finally had saved enough money to start the paperwork for a divorce. Though stunned, Eva acted quickly to sabotage Annie's plan.

"We were discussing it downstairs," Eva said. "Then I went upstairs where she had taken her pocketbook. I opened it and took the money out. I went to the store and bought her four or five dresses to keep her from getting the divorce. I even took the price tags off so she couldn't take them back. That delayed that. She just fell across the bed when she realized what I had done and laughed and cried."

"I don't know what I'm going to do with you," Annie said to Eva.

Eva: "You and Robert can make it."

"Yeah," Annie said, "we can make it, but I just don't want to anymore."

Whirlwind and Peggy spent those four years at Meharry in near isolation. He rarely went home because he didn't want to deal with his family's disapproval of his personal life. He never contacted any of his old friends and didn't try to make any new ones. Getting the medical degree was his No. 1 goal; keeping Peggy by his side wasn't far behind. He wrote Annie occasionally during that time. His message rarely varied: Let me go. He once listed 67 reasons why she should divorce him.

A reason not listed—falling in love with another man—helped Annie move on. At the height of her dismay, Annie, with Robert Jr. by her side, went home to Goldsboro, where she worked for two years as a teacher's aide. Lonely and vulnerable, she spent much of her spare time as a church volunteer. Reverend James C. Taylor, the minister who had married Annie and Robert in 1922, often consoled her and treated her with respect. In the process, Taylor, who had become a bishop in the Methodist church, also re-ignited in her a passion to love again. He promised to marry her, a vow that made it far easier for Annie to look beyond the embarrassing and dreaded process of divorce to a brighter, happier future.

At the time, Papa Jerry was as oblivious to his son's troubled marriage as he was to the economic turmoil that struck the nation near the end of the 1920s. In 1929, while the stock market crumbled, Papa Jerry rode a wave of prosperity. He moved his family into more spacious living quarters: the Stubbs House on Fourth Street in Plymouth. Named for

William H. Stubbs, whose family lived there from the fall of 1886 until 1919, the mansion-sized home, situated on a square block of land, was the largest house in the area. It was a white, two-story structure with a porch on each level. Four bedrooms were on the upper level, each warmed by separate fireplaces. A wide hallway ran the length of the house on the lower level where there were two bedrooms, a dining room and a den. The house was purchased in Mama Nancy's name.

Folklore says the house, built in 1830, was used as a hospital during the Civil War because it was out of range of Yankee gun ships moored in the Roanoke River. More than anything else, the house symbolized Papa Jerry's status as a successful businessman. His achievement was all the more remarkable since it occurred in Plymouth, a segregated community, and while the Great Depression consumed the nation.

In the late 1920s, Papa Jerry built an auditorium in downtown Plymouth. He named it "Dreamland." Talking movies were shown upstairs, and a restaurant was on the lower level. It was one of only a few places families could go for an afternoon of entertainment. Despite the depression, Dreamland thrived when it opened.

Whirlwind graduated from Meharry in 1932. So relieved to have realized his dream, he didn't bother to attend the graduation ceremony. Besides, he knew memories of Meharry wouldn't measure up to his memories of his undergraduate football days at Lincoln.

The next year, he began an internship at Prairie View Hospital in Prairie View, Texas. During the year, he learned that Annie had indeed severed their relationship and had married Bishop Taylor. Even though he repeatedly had begged her to file for divorce, Whirlwind was stunned when he learned that she actually had gone through with it. Once when Annie and Bishop Taylor were on vacation, Whirlwind went to Goldsboro and snatched Robert Jr. away from his grandmother. Annie chose not to force him to return the six-year-old boy.

Soon afterward, Whirlwind married Peggy in New York. He took her to Plymouth in the summer of 1933 for the first time to meet his family. Not everyone in the Johnson family knew about the other woman in Whirlwind's life. When Whirlwind's youngest brother, 10-year-old Rupert, was introduced to Peggy, he asked his brother, "What, you have another wife?"

A NEW WIFE

Papa Jerry had been kept in the dark, too. He had no idea that Annie no longer was a part of Whirlwind's life. Whirlwind discussed his personal life with Mama Nancy, never with Papa Jerry.

Papa Jerry's initial conversation with Peggy was quite short and blunt:

"Do you know Annie?"

"Yes," Peggy responded.

"Well, she'll always be first in our lives," Papa Jerry said.

Shortly after that exchange, one of his daughters pulled Papa Jerry to the side and admonished him for embarrassing his son's new wife.

Abrasive comments were exchanged from time to time in the Johnson household, but they were a close family. Disagreements or disappointments rarely caused family members to avoid one another. Family affairs and special celebrations always were important occasions. Whirlwind especially looked forward to going to Plymouth every April 16 so he and Papa Jerry could enjoy joint birthday celebrations.

Whirlwind's new role as the doctor in the family immediately elevated his position as a family leader. In a few short years, even Papa Jerry, the family's highly successful businessman, would have to take a back seat to Whirlwind in shaping decisions regarding family matters. It didn't matter that Whirlwind would establish his practice in a neighboring state.

Whirlwind Johnson, then 33, with Peggy and Robert Jr. in tow, slipped behind the wheel of his new 1933 Buick and headed for western Virginia. They were on course to make new friends and neighbors and build a new life together in Lynchburg, a city situated on seven hills.

Small Town Doctor

WHIRLWIND WAS IN PEAK physical condition when he left Lincoln to coach Virginia Seminary College in Lynchburg in 1924, and during that time, there was nothing he enjoyed more—except maybe the pleasure of a woman's company—than to tuck that ball under his arms in scrimmages against his varsity players and smash through the line to the end zone. He left Lynchburg a year later with a treasure chest of fond memories, but he'd also tucked away a bit of information that would bring him back nine years later, carrying a doctor's bag, instead of a football.

As Virginia Seminary's coach in 1924, Whirlwind remembered having difficulty finding a doctor whenever a player was seriously injured in a scrimmage or game. White doctors attended neither the scrimmages nor the games, and the town's lone black doctor only made occasional appearances. Nine years later, when Whirlwind learned that Lynchburg's black doctor had died, he decided that the town was an ideal place to establish his medical practice.

When Whirlwind left Plymouth for Lynchburg, Mama Nancy gave him enough money to pay for food and rent for two months. He wouldn't have lasted without it.

"No one called on Robert at all during those first two months," his sister Victoria said, drifting into a vivid account of Whirlwind's slow start as Lynchburg's new black physician:

He used to walk the streets, go back home and still no calls. He was living on Wise Street at the time. Then one day, a little Negro girl in the neighborhood took sick. Her parents called a white doctor, but he couldn't do nothing for her. Then the white doctor said, 'Understand y'all got a colored doctor down on the corner. Why don't you give him a try?'

They called Robert and asked him to come over to look at their child. He did. When he got to the house, the child seemed to be in a coma. Then a vision of Mama came before Robert. He thought about something he'd seen Mama do. He asked the lady if she had a piece of Octagon soap. He took some soap and gave her an enema. Pretty soon, her bowels moved and, finally, she woke up. The parents were so happy. They wanted to know how much he charged.

Well, he didn't have a penny in his pocket, except for a dollar left from the money Mama gave him. He said, 'I'm not going to charge you one penny. Just let me stay here through the night to see how she reacts. And if she's okay, tell your neighbors to give me a call whenever they need a doctor.' That little girl was his first patient.

Victoria kept a picture of Mama Nancy, with a dollar bill inside the frame, for many years on a table in her bedroom. An inscription on a piece of brown tape attached to the dollar read: "In memory of Mama."

"That was the last dollar Robert had from the money Mama gave him when he went to Lynchburg," Victoria said. "He put it in that frame with Mama's picture."

It took Whirlwind less than a year to gain the confidence and respect of Lynchburg's black community. He possessed the ideal attributes needed by a small town doctor. His outgoing, easy manner made patients feel at ease and confident in his care. He responded to calls for help regardless of the day or time.

"He was a person who would take you for a drive in his car if he thought you needed a little relaxation," said Mattie Robinson, a teacher who, along with two others, shared a room in Whirlwind's home during the 1933-34 school year. "I never had to go to him for any illness, but everybody thought he was a marvelous doctor. People liked him because he was very friendly, very jovial, just a nice person to be around."

Whirlwind's practice grew rapidly, prompting him to hire a staff and expand his workspace. Black physicians were denied privileges at Lynchburg's only hospital; so Whirlwind established a clinic, which included several examining rooms. Just as he shared his expertise in football as a coach, Whirlwind did the same in medicine. He invited young physicians who had recently completed medical school, or who had not yet received a license, to practice under his guidance in Lynchburg.

Leon Braswell, an Omega Psi Phi fraternity brother at Lincoln, was the first of a half dozen who began their careers as physicians in Whirlwind's Lynchburg clinic. James Smith, Arthur Gregg and Ralph Boulware were among the others. Each stayed with Whirlwind and his family briefly when they first arrived. He gave them room and board and provided them with salaries as well.

Beginning in January 1945, Whirlwind spent six months in Wilmington, North Carolina, learning obstetrics and techniques in minor surgery from a friend, Dr. Hubert Eaton Sr., who, at the time, was chief surgeon at an all-black hospital. During those six months, Dr. Boulware, who was Dr. Eaton's brother-in-law, took over Whirlwind's practice in Lynchburg. When Whirlwind returned, Dr. Boulware went back to medical school for further credits. In 1949, he established a separate practice in Lynchburg.

"Whirlwind and I had a good working relationship," Dr. Boulware said. "If he wasn't going to be in town, he'd tell his patients to call me in case of emergencies. If I had to be away, I'd tell my patients to call him. We just worked that way all the time."

In the 1940s, doctor's fees were $3.00 for house calls and $2.00 for office visits. But lack of money never prevented Whirlwind from treating patients in need.

"He was a kind physician, a good physician," Dr. Boulware said. "Even if his patients couldn't pay him, he gave them the best of care."

One of Whirlwind's relatives added, "So many people didn't have the money to pay him; so they would give him preserves, and he appreciated that more than he did money. He didn't turn down any food."

Housing patterns in some parts of Lynchburg were racially mixed, but Jim Crow laws kept the races separate in public gatherings and institutions. Black and white youngsters attended separate schools, and all other public facilities, including hospitals, were segregated. However, with talent and a strong work ethic that he seemed to have inherited from Papa Jerry, Whirlwind transcended the racial barriers of his time. Some white families living in Whirlwind's neighborhood called on him, especially for treatment related to unwanted pregnancies or embarrassing social diseases.

"He had quite a few white patients," Dr. Boulware said. "They used to tell him what the white physicians were saying about him."

In 1936, Whirlwind moved his family from the modest house on Wise Street into a spacious two-story home at 1422 Pierce St., which was located in a predominantly white neighborhood. The brown and white frame house was twice the size of any other house on the block. It included just enough land to build something Whirlwind considered a necessity: a tennis court. He constructed a clay court in his backyard, and tennis became an integral part of his life. After a long day at the office, an hour or so on the court was as much a part of his routine as eating dinner, which came after his workout on the court.

Whirlwind had played tennis casually at Shaw and at Lincoln, but he became addicted to the game while serving his internship at Prairie View Hospital. Then 33, he no longer could dazzle anyone with speed and shifty moves on the football field, and while attending medical school, he learned that his active, athletic life caused him to develop larger than normal heart muscles. He believed that keeping active helped him stay healthy.

Prairie View had an excellent tennis program, and Whirlwind learned that one could not master the genteel sport with athletic ability alone. He learned the nuances of the game by playing with more skilled players. Few blacks played tennis in Lynchburg and segregation prevented him from playing with whites at public facilities. He found camaraderie and competitiveness with other black professionals who also were attracted to tennis. Through his friend Dr. Eaton, Whirlwind became acquainted with a group of black professionals from North Carolina in 1936.

"My first contact with Whirlwind Johnson was through tennis," Dr. Eaton said. "He was a friend of Lionel Cook of Durham. And here in North Carolina, we had a group of tennis players who were (working) professionals. We would rotate from city to city every Sunday. Each of us had our own court in our backyards. We'd play in Durham, in Raleigh and several times, we'd play in Smithfield, North Carolina, with Dr. C.W. Furlonge. And we'd come here to Wilmington. There weren't many of us, about a half a dozen. I believe Whirlwind got the information from Cook that we were playing; so he invited us to his house in Lynchburg and said he'd like to join us."

The sessions with his fellow professionals became the highlight of Whirlwind's social life. He was delighted to have found this group of friends who shared his interest and enthusiasm for the sport.

"He would have given anything to have been able to raise his game on the tennis court to the highest level," Dr. Eaton said. "But as an athlete, he knew it would take more time and work than he could spare. His personal game was of deep concern to him."

The following summer, a family tragedy caused Whirlwind to take his eye and his mind off the tennis ball for a while. Papa Jerry had continued the tradition of letting his sons earn money and working experience as members of his logging crew. Samuel DeLeon, one of Whirlwind's younger brothers, was 18 when he was killed during a logging mishap. He was helping load logs on a barge in the Roanoke River when the barge began to sink.

"They must have overloaded the barge," said Rupert, Whirlwind's youngest brother. "Samuel and a few other guys tried to save the barge by taking some of the logs off, but it was too late. So they jumped off and started swimming to shore. One guy—they called him Shorty—stayed on the barge because he couldn't swim. Samuel went back to save him, but when he got there the logs toppled over and mashed him against the barge."

Shorty was saved, but Samuel was the first and only person Papa Jerry lost in more than 40 years as a logging contractor. Soon after burying his son, Papa Jerry retired from the logging business. Robert returned to Lynchburg more determined than ever to balance a demanding work schedule with adequate physical recreation. It was a time in history when blacks began to make noticeable gains as superstar athletes in the world's sports arenas.

Though admired mainly for showmanship and remarkable antics, the Harlem Globetrotters, formed by Abe Saperstein in 1927, were a major attraction wherever they played. Jesse Owens ran away with four gold medals in the 1936 Olympics, held in Germany. Snubbed by German Chancellor Adolph Hitler, Owens won the admiration of most

Americans. In 1937, Joe Louis, nicknamed the Brown Bomber, knocked out Jim Braddock to become the world's heavyweight boxing champion.

Robert's glory years at Lincoln gave him a taste of superstardom, albeit on a smaller stage. His Lincoln teammates and others who saw him play often talked of his exploits in the superlative and made him feel as if he was the greatest player of his time. He might have been.

His success on the gridiron instilled within him a hunger and a strong desire to excel in every arena, even on the tennis court. He looked forward to his regular sessions with his fellow professionals, but knew that they were not enough. Through them, he learned of a black tennis organization that sponsored national and other events, mainly in major cities along the eastern seaboard. The organization was called the American Tennis Association (ATA).

8

History of the ATA

COMPETITION AMONG WHIRLWIND's group of black professionals grew keener every year. Still, Whirlwind and the others knew that the expertise demonstrated at the group's round-robin tournaments paled in comparison to that on display at white tournaments. Tennis had been a white man's sport since its inception.

The first lawn tennis tournament, featuring whites in white pants, was held in 1877 outside London, at the All England Croquet and Lawn Tennis Club in Wimbledon. Played under rules devised three years earlier by Major Walter Clopton Wingfield, men's singles was the only event. Wimbledon added men's doubles and women's singles in 1884 and women's doubles and mixed doubles in 1913.

The first lawn tennis championship tournament played on U.S. soil in 1881 was held under the auspices of the United States National Lawn Tennis Association (later the USLTA and now the USTA). Men's singles and doubles were the only events played. Women's singles was added in 1887, women's doubles in 1889 and mixed doubles in 1892. For the most part, the game was played on private courts at exclusive country clubs, where gentlemen of wealth and their sophisticated and stylish women fostered a spirit of wholesome competition, sportsmanship and fair play.

Tennis belonged to the nation's white aristocracy until the turn of the century, when concrete and clay courts were constructed on playgrounds, at high schools and on college campuses. The game was opened to the public, except, of course, for blacks, who were not allowed to play at public parks or white schools and were allowed to enter white country clubs only for menial jobs, such as kitchen helpers, maids or servants.

There was, however, great interest in the sport among the black elite. Black doctors, college professors and businessmen mimicked the practices of wealthy whites, including their mannerisms, habits and leisure activities. If tennis tournaments provided wealthy whites with special enjoyment and camaraderie, then surely they would do as much for wealthy blacks.

Blacks held their first interstate tournament in 1898 at the Chautauqua Tennis Club in Philadelphia. By 1916, matches were scheduled periodically among 58 black tennis clubs scattered across the country. Generally, players from Massachusetts; Washington, D.C.; New York; New Jersey; and Pennsylvania participated in these events. A plan to establish an annual national tournament was discussed in the spring of 1916 at a New York meeting. Invitations were sent to all the black clubs. Twenty clubs sent representatives to an organizing committee, which met Nov. 30, 1916—Thanksgiving Day—in Washington, D.C. When the meeting ended, the American Tennis Association (ATA) was born. No reference was made to race in the title because the organizers didn't want to exclude whites from participating.

The organization's objectives were:

- To bring colored tennis enthusiasts and players into closer and friendly relations,
- To improve the standards of existing clubs,
- To encourage the formation of new clubs,
- To hold an annual national championship tournament,
- To regulate the dates of local and regional tournaments to avoid conflicts,
- To appoint referees and officials for each event, and
- To promote the standard of the game among colored men.

The ATA's founding fathers included Dr. Harry S. McCard, Dr. William H. Wright, Dr. B.M. Rhetta and Ralph Cook of Baltimore; Dr. Henry Freeman, John F.N. Wilkinson and Tally Holmes of Washington,

D.C.; Dr. D. Ivison Hoage, Julius Rainford, H.W. Heron and Gerald F. Norman of New York; James T. Howard of Philadelphia; and Howard M. Smith of Kansas City. Dr. McCard was the organization's first president and Norman was elected executive secretary.

The first ATA National Championships, consisting of three events, were held at Druid Hill Park in Baltimore in August 1917. Tally Holmes won the men's singles title, Lucy Stowe won the women's crown and Holmes and Sylvester Smith were the ATA's first national doubles champions. Boys' singles, women's doubles and mixed doubles were added in 1924. Russell Smith won the first boys' title, Isadore Channels and Emma Leonard took the first women's doubles title, and Nellie Nicholson and Dr. B.M. Rhetta were the first mixed doubles titleholders.

Interest in tennis among non-professional blacks grew steadily in the 1920s. The ATA was incorporated in 1926, the same year Eyre Saitch, an outstanding basketball player with the Harlem Rens, showed his versatility by capturing the ATA men's singles title. Meanwhile, the East Coast clubs, which had hosted the annual national tournament, couldn't accommodate the increasing number of participants. ATA officials were delighted by the growth, but troubled by the inadequacy of their club facilities. A few of the nation's historically black colleges provided the solution to their problem.

By the 1920s, many of the black colleges founded after the Civil War had become an integral part of black life. Major black social events, such as dances, fashion shows and debutante balls, were held on college campuses. Hampton Institute, Morehouse College and Lincoln University offered tennis as part of their physical education curricula before 1910. Other black colleges followed suit.

The marriage of the ATA and black colleges proved to be mutually beneficial. The ATA needed more tennis courts and sites that could provide more housing space; the black colleges desired the affiliation with ATA members, wealthy and well-respected professionals, who might provide additional funding. Beginning in 1927, the ATA held its national championships on various black college campuses. The event became a social extravaganza as much as an athletic contest. Dances, fashion shows and other activities were scheduled during the week of play.

"We played at Hampton, Tuskegee, Lincoln, South Carolina State and Central State in Wilberforce, Ohio," said Clifford Blackman, an ATA member/official since its inception. "We traveled in cars; that was the only way we could get around. We had quite a lot of opposition from the USLTA. They were very uppity. They didn't allow Negroes to play in their tournaments."

While the national event moved from campus to campus, the champions in the early years often were the same. Tally Holmes and Edgar G. Brown each won four men's singles titles during the first 12 years. Dr. Reginald Weir became the first player to win the men's title three consecutive years (1931-33). Isadore Channels, Lula Ballard and Flora Lomax each won four women's singles titles, but Ora Washington, a gracious smooth-stroking woman, was the dominant woman player of the 1930s. Washington won a record seven consecutive (1929-35) ATA national women's titles. She won an eighth title in 1937. Later, Althea Gibson, with 10 consecutive titles (1947-56), broke Washington's records for most consecutive titles and most titles.

William "Big Bill" Tilden of Philadelphia and Helen "Little Miss Poker Face" Wills Moody of Berkeley, California, helped stir greater interest in tennis among whites in the 1920s and 1930s. As an amateur, Tilden won 138 of 192 tournaments played, lost only 28 finals and had a remarkable 907-62 match record. With a cannonball serve and hard-driving ground strokes, Tilden won 10 Grand Slam tournament titles, including six consecutive U.S. championships (1920-25). Tilden, who turned pro in 1931, was inducted into the International Tennis Hall of Fame in 1959.

During a 20-year career (1919-38), Moody, who played with an unflappable demeanor, won 52 of 92 tournaments played and had a 398-35 match record. She won 19 Grand Slam tournament titles, including a record eight Wimbledon singles titles. (Martina Navratilova eclipsed Moody's Wimbledon record in 1990, defeating Zina Garrison for her ninth Wimbledon singles crown.) Moody also won seven U.S. titles and four French crowns. She was inducted into the International Tennis Hall of Fame in 1969. Black champions of that era yearned to test their skills against the top white players, but they were barred from amateur and pro events.

A breakthrough of sorts occurred in 1940, however, when Wilson

WHIRLWIND

Sporting Goods Company President L.B. Icely arranged to have J. Donald Budge, the first player to win the Grand Slam (Australian, French, Wimbledon and U.S. titles in the same calendar year), meet ATA champion Jimmie McDaniel in an exhibition.

The match was played July 29, 1940 at New York's Cosmopolitan Tennis Club before more than 2,000 fans. The match drew media attention from black and white newspapers, but was considered a major event mainly in the black community. Bleachers flanked the court on both sides and every seat was occupied. Some people who lived near the court watched from fire escapes and from windows in surrounding buildings. Those unable to see listened to the score, which was announced on a public address system.

Budge, who was then a professional, defeated McDaniel, then a student at Xavier University in New Orleans, 6-1, 6-2. According to newspaper reports, Budge was "perfectly at ease . . . handling his shots with accuracy and composure."

Facing the man considered the best in the world, McDaniel understandably had the jitters. He committed 13 double faults and numerous other unforced errors. Al Laney of the *New York Herald Tribune* wrote: "It is not quite fair to McDaniel or to Negro tennis in general to judge by this one match. It must be remembered that he was playing before his own people as their champion against a man nobody in the world can beat."

Budge appreciated McDaniel's situation and commended him on his skills, despite his sub par effort. Addressing the crowd through a loudspeaker, Budge said: "Jimmy is a very good player. I'd say he'd rank with the first 10 of our white players. And with some more practice against players like me, maybe he could some day beat all of them."

After the singles match, Budge, who was working for Icely at the Wilson Sporting Goods Company, teamed with Dr. Reginald Weir to play a doubles exhibition against McDaniel and Richard Cohen. Cohen and Weir were the reigning ATA doubles champions. Icely also arranged for Charles E. Hare, a former British Davis Cup player, to meet Harold Mitchell of the ATA in an exhibition match at Tuskegee Institute in Alabama. That match was played at the ATA Nationals in 1941, the year the organization celebrated its Silver Jubilee.

In a letter to the ATA, Holcombe Ward, president of the USLTA, wrote: "It is indeed a pleasure to congratulate the ATA and its officers at this period of its history. On behalf of the organization which I represent, I extend most cordial greetings and sincere wishes for the success of the American Tennis Association in its further development, work and efforts to maintain the high standards of the game of tennis wherever played."

Ward, however, didn't invite ATA members to play in USLTA events. Those doors remained closed to blacks.

9

Other Loves

By 1940, the ATA, an organization that had begun with 25 clubs and more than 100 members, had grown to include 145 clubs with more than 1,000 members. Six clubs were established in Bermuda. The Budge vs. McDaniel exhibition helped grow the genteel sport among blacks, as did word-of-mouth marketing and the generosity of wealthy ATA members, including Whirlwind.

Led by New Yorkers—Dr. D. Ivison Hoage, president, and Bertram Baker, executive secretary—the ATA had 11 field officers selected to promote the game and recruit new members. Whirlwind was the ATA's Middle Atlantic field secretary. He had assumed control of the Hill City Recreation Club in Lynchburg a few years earlier and had paid the dues and other fees that allowed the club to become an ATA member. His wife, Peggy, was listed as the club's secretary.

Whirlwind taught neighbors and friends to play tennis and continued weekly sessions with his North Carolina buddies. His game, however, stayed the same despite the increased time on court, as well as his time spent devouring page after page of instructional material about the game. Determined to become a stronger player, Whirlwind expanded his search for stronger competition by recruiting ringers and rising stars from everywhere. They stayed at his house during the summer months at his expense, as long as they completed a single chore: play a set or two with the host at his convenience.

Bennie Sides, a hard-hitting youngster from Chicago, spent a summer with Whirlwind. Nat Jackson, the 1934 ATA men's singles champion, was a frequent visitor. Even though his exposure to tennis was relatively limited, Whirlwind was an astute judge of athletic talent. His years as a top athlete and coach made him aware of the need to consider personality and other intangibles when assessing a player's potential.

He preferred to teach players who followed his directions without deviation and who demonstrated respect for discipline. He found women to be more malleable than men. While serving his internship at Prairie View, Whirlwind met Agnes Lawson, a young woman with strong athletic ability, but weak in fundamentals. In 1940, Whirlwind also invited her to spend a summer at his home to work on her game. Lawson, who accepted his invitation, ended the summer on a high note by capturing the ATA national women's title.

Family business matters kept Whirlwind shuffling to and from Plymouth, even during the summer, his peak tennis playing months. To make his trips to Plymouth a bit more enjoyable, Whirlwind built a tennis court next to Papa Jerry's Dreamland Auditorium, which had closed as the Great Depression wore on. Whirlwind sponsored a tournament there and brought in top players from Virginia and other parts of North Carolina. During the weekend tournament, Whirlwind re-opened Dreamland as a nightclub. With money never a concern, Whirlwind's entertainment packages included the top black bands of that era. Bob Brown's band from Norfolk was the opening night act. Other big bands playing Plymouth's hot spot included the Trenton Nighthawks and the Dixie Play Girls, an all-female band. With help from family members, Whirlwind managed Dreamland from Lynchburg, making twice-a-month weekend trips during summers.

The cooler months made it easier for Whirlwind to spend more time in Plymouth. He loved tennis passionately, but it was a seasonal love, lasting each year from May to September. Indoor tennis courts were scarce in the early years and very few players enjoyed working up a sweat in frigid weather. Each year after Labor Day, Whirlwind slipped on his rubber boots and hunting jacket, grabbed one of his shotguns, and then trekked through the woods in search of a different kind of trophy.

With bird dogs dancing at his feet, Whirlwind hunted fowl, rabbits, squirrels, raccoons and muskrat. Sometimes, he'd go deep into the countryside to hunt deer and other big game.

"Without any question hunting was Whirlwind's second love," Dr. Eaton said. "He liked to fish, too, but hunting came first. He was an outdoorsman."

Edison Louis Towe, Jr. was among several young men in Plymouth who waited eagerly to accompany Whirlwind on weekend fishing excursions. "Couple of times when he came down, he didn't have access to a boat," Towe said. "I had one at the time, and we went out and fished up the Roanoke River, other rivers and also out in the Albermarle Sound. I didn't go out in the ocean with him. Whenever we went fishing, Doc would have stacks of magazines. He always carried something to read and he was always influential, trying to give youngsters sound advice."

Papa Jerry often took his older son to hunt in Oak City, near Williamston, and to fish up the James River. Whirlwind occasionally took Robert Jr. to hunt or fish, hoping that their father-son bond would grow stronger. But Robert Jr. found more agony than enjoyment during those early morning ventures.

"When I was 12, I recall him taking me fishing a lot," Robert Jr. said. "I hated it. We would get up at 4 a.m. and he would tell me that we'd be home by noon. We never got back before 6 p.m., and all we had to eat was cornbread and fish, if we caught any. I went hunting with him one time wearing blue jeans. He had on a hunting outfit with rubber boots. Who do you think got cold? I was mad and said to myself, 'If I ever get out of this, I'll never do it again.'"

When he wasn't on a hunting or fishing trip, Whirlwind often spent weekends with his first love, football, as an official and sometimes as a spectator. He used to referee local high school games on Friday nights and traveled short distances to officiate CIAA games on Saturday afternoons. Occasionally, he'd spend Sunday afternoons in Washington, D.C., watching the Washington Redskins.

Whirlwind went to Washington one weekend in 1941 to see Lincoln play Howard University in a Homecoming game. There, he befriended Dr. W. Henry "Stud" Greene, a Howard graduate and D.C.-based physician, at the alumni dance.

OTHER LOVES

"I founded a mental rest club that me, Whirlwind and a few other professionals belonged to," Greene said. "In those days, the deadline for filing income tax was March 15. Every week after income taxes were filed, the mental rest club would take a trip together. The first year, which was 1942, we went to the Kentucky Derby. Couldn't stay in any hotels down there, so we leased a friend's house. The idea of the mental health club was to rest the mind, not the body.

"We'd stay up all night, playing cards, running the streets, drinking whisky. Practically all of us were physicians, but this was the only week during the year that we didn't have to go to the office or worry about our patients. We went to Whirlwind's family home in Plymouth one year. We went to Miami; New Orleans for the Mardi Gras; Havana, Cuba. We pledged to maybe die hungry, but to never die tired from overworking."

Most members of the mental rest club were married, but wives never accompanied them on their trips. It was a bachelor's week out, and on more than one occasion, these well-respected professionals shoved conservative ways aside and let silliness prevail. During a trip to Miami Beach, the group nearly got evicted from its motel because of rowdiness.

"We had been out for a night on the town in Miami Beach," Greene said. "We put one of the guys out of the cab and made him walk back to the motel. I believe it was Carter Marshall. When Carter got back, he brought a stray dog to the motel and thought he was putting it in Leo Roberts' room. Instead, he had put it in the landlady's room. She was some kind of mad when that dog started barking and running around the room.

"The next morning, she put a note on everybody's door to vacate by 6 p.m. Everybody got a note but Whirlwind. He had gotten in good with the landlady by sending her flowers and writing her notes every day we were there. She didn't put a note on his door. He finally convinced her not to kick us out."

Occasionally, the group's entertainment involved high stakes gambling sessions. "We used to play a lot of tonk, hearts and poker," Greene said. "I have seen Whirlwind and another doctor sit beside each other and bet up to $500 that their next card would be higher than the other's. Whirlwind loved to play poker. They hooked him once in Norfolk.

Brought in a ringer and set a trap for him. Beat him out of close to $8,000."

Gambling with some friends in Wilmington, North Carolina, Whirlwind once lost his car in a poker game. One of his buddies gave him enough money to catch a Greyhound bus back to Lynchburg. Whether they knew him as an athlete, physician or neighbor, many of Whirlwind's male friends say that besides a powerful passion for tennis, his main 'other love' was a pretty woman.

"Sure I knew Whirlwind," a lifelong friend once said. "He stole my woman!"

In a seemingly lifelong pursuit of beautiful women, Whirlwind was rarely slowed by the presence of wedding bands—on his finger or theirs.

One of Whirlwind's Lynchburg friends said, "Let me tell you what he'd do. He'd see somebody with a beautiful girl and he would pull her to the side and say, 'Look, he can't do for you what I can do. I can give you diamonds and furs. I can take you to Miami Beach or the Bahamas.' And he would do everything he said he would do. Now, what woman is going to turn down something like that?"

James McCrea, a Lincoln classmate, said: "Whirlwind did everything intensely. He played football intensely, he played tennis and poker intensely, and he loved women intensely."

Though married, pretty women routinely were included in Robert's social outings. He occasionally showed up at CIAA basketball tournaments with a pretty woman on each arm. He escorted model-like figures to Redskin football games, to the Penn Relays in Pennsylvania and to tennis tournaments from Boston to Miami. He favored the fair-skinned ladies; it was the custom of that time.

In a poignant passage in *The Souls of Black Folks,* published in 1903, author W.E.B. DuBois proclaimed, "The problem of the 20th century is the problem of the color line." DuBois understood that a class system based on skin color would be damaging to the black psyche at least for the rest of the century. By the late '20s, blacks recognized that more than anything else, the "color line" was a barrier to the American mainstream. Many blacks who wrestled with the realities of racism on a daily basis came to believe that looking white might be the next best thing.

OTHER LOVES

Some black men, especially entertainers, processed their hair to make it wavy-white. Black women used hot combs and chemicals to make their kinky hair soft and curly. Members of both sexes used creams and other makeup to lighten their skin and to hide or soften the impact of their big noses and full lips.

Lena Horne, Cab Calloway, Billie Eckstine and Billie Holiday were among the black entertainers of that era who had the white look of approval that many blacks strove to achieve. With few exceptions (Nat King Cole and Bill "Bojangles" Robinson among them), the truly successful black entertainer seldom bore the physical traits—dark skin, kinky hair, full lips—that marked his African ancestors. Ahoskie, North Carolina, and Poquoson, Virginia, were among several Southern cities where light-skinned blacks married family members, determined to insure that future generations also would be light-skinned. Dark-complexioned blacks were made to feel unwelcome in such cities. Some fair-skinned mothers used to tell their children to "wash their children's faces and comb their hair" *before* choosing a spouse. Trying to "look white" got blacks in trouble only when they got caught passing for white.

Concern about one's complexion wasn't confined to the South. Dr. George Cannon, one of Whirlwind's classmates at Lincoln, recalled going to a social club in New York, the Convivial Coterie, in the 1920s. Cannon, who was light brown, said he took a light-skinned black woman to a dance at the club. When he tried to date her again, she refused.

"She told me that the club members told her not to date me again because I was too black," Cannon said.

Dr. Hildrus A. Poindexter, who was Whirlwind's teammate at Lincoln and a foremost expert on the treatment of tropical diseases, encountered a similar experience in Washington, D.C. Poindexter, who was dark brown, remembered receiving an award presented by a D.C. club, The Blue Vein Society, in the 1930s. The club members were all light-skinned women.

"I remember dancing with one of the members of the club after the award was presented," Poindexter said. "She was light-skinned. She asked if I was married and I said, 'Yes, my wife came with me.' And she said, 'Oh, you mean you married the dark-skinned one over there?' I was so insulted I just walked off the floor and left her standing.

"Light-skinned women didn't mind marrying a dark-skinned professional man, and it was considered a badge of success among dark-skinned men to marry a very fair girl. The attitude was, 'Why settle for anything less than the best?' And the yellow women were considered the best."

As Lynchburg's most prominent black physician, Whirlwind had his choice of women and sampled every type. Whirlwind's friendships among his male cohorts seemed as important to him. Even when they weren't on a "mental rest" break, Whirlwind and his male companions spent time together. Dr. Greene didn't play tennis, but occasionally, he visited Whirlwind in Lynchburg to watch him play. In 1946, Greene and a few of Whirlwind's other non-tennis playing friends went to Central State University in Wilberforce, Ohio, to watch Whirlwind play in the ATA National Championships.

"They put us out of the bleachers because we were raising hell, yelling for Whirlwind during his match," Greene said. "The security police told us we had to leave. So we went up into the dormitory where we were staying and could see Whirlwind playing from there. We started yelling and screaming again."

Whirlwind lost the match despite his friends' clamorous support. Still, Whirlwind's cohorts helped make that year's ATA quite memorable. However, a young Harlem girl turned Whirlwind's head more than once, but not for the usual reason.

Dr. Eaton and Whirlwind spent hours watching an 18-year-old lanky girl from New York move easily through the women's draw. They sat together in the bleachers on the last day of the tournament watching a very raw, but clearly talented Althea Gibson play New Jersey's Roumania Peters in the women's final.

10

Aiding Althea

SITTING HIGH IN THE BLEACHERS, the two well-dressed doctors watched lanky Althea Gibson battle little Roumania Peters in the ATA National women's final. Occasionally, they spoke to one another in hushed tones, as if they were devising a treatment plan for a patient. In a sense, Whirlwind and Dr. Eaton were indeed collaborating on a prescription designed to rescue 18-year-old Althea from the crime-infested streets of Harlem.

"Whirlwind said to me, 'You know, Hubert, I wish we could do something to help that girl, Althea,'" Eaton said. "She's a good tennis player, but she's not going to amount to much doing what she's doing now, hanging around on the streets of New York."

Though erratic and undisciplined, Gibson impressed the doctors with her power and tenacity. The doctors concurred that Gibson would need polishing on the court as well as off court.

"She's got good moves, but she seems to lose concentration, occasionally," Eaton said.

Fred Johnson, a one-armed pro, who taught at New York's Cosmopolitan Club, gave Gibson her first lesson in 1941, when she was 14. A year later, she won her first title, defeating Nina Irwin, a white girl, in the final of an ATA event. During the next few years, Gibson was the dominant junior girl on the ATA circuit. In 1944, the 17-year-old gifted athlete captured the ATA National girls' singles crown. In 1946, Cosmopolitan Club supporters sent her to the ATA Nationals at Central

State University in Wilberforce, Ohio, where Whirlwind and Dr. Eaton watched her lose to Peters 6-4, 7-9, 6-3 in the final.

The loss caused neither Whirlwind nor Eaton to waver in their belief that Gibson had a touch of greatness in her racket swing. Turning to Whirlwind, Eaton said, "What do you think we ought to do?"

"I don't know," Whirlwind replied.

Then Eaton offered his plan: "I tell you what. I don't have anybody to practice with down in Wilmington, except Nat Jackson. If she's willing to come, if her mother gives her permission, I'll take her down to Wilmington to live with my family and let her finish high school. You keep her during the summer and see to it that she gets to the tournaments. I have a little different practice than yours. I do obstetrics and surgery. I can't be away for a long time like you can."

Whirlwind said, "That sounds all right. I'll be willing to participate in something like that."

The doctors then tossed the ball in Althea's court.

"Immediately after Althea got through playing, she was standing around talking to some people," Eaton said. "We went up to her and said, 'Althea, we want to talk to you as soon as you have a moment.' We told her that we had been watching her play, observing her for more than just that one time, and we thought she had excellent potentiality. But we had made some inquiries and found out that she wasn't in school. She would start school, and then jump out. We told her we had made some plans to help her with her education and at the same time, help her with her tennis. 'Are you interested?'"

"Who wouldn't be interested in a deal like that?" Althea responded.

Eaton, continuing the story, said, "The understanding was that she would go back to New York and have her mother write a letter giving Althea permission to come and stay with my family. This she did and I got the letter a few days before Althea arrived in Wilmington."

Gibson, who was born on a cotton farm in Silver, South Carolina, on August 25, 1927, moved with her family to New York when she was three years old. She spent her formative years growing up on the rugged streets of Harlem and made the transition from farm girl to city girl without missing a step. She excelled in baseball, basketball, even football. She was unbeatable in paddle tennis and was a stickball champion in the Police Athletic League. Former New York Mayor David Dinkins said Gibson was playing a smart, aggressive game of table tennis when he first met her in the mid-'40s at a social club in Scotch Plains, New Jersey. "I called her champ then and to this very day, I call her champ," Dinkins said.

A tough tomboy as a teen, she also had the instincts of a boxer and demeanor of a hustler. When not involved in tennis or team athletics, Althea spent most of her teenage years in pool halls and bowling alleys. Once she moved away from Harlem, she quickly learned that life with Dr. Eaton and Dr. Johnson would involve more than a change of scenery.

After graduating from high school in Wilmington, North Carolina, in 1949, Gibson attended Florida A&M University and finished with a degree in physical education. Insofar as the social graces were concerned, Althea's life with her two doctors was quite a learning experience. Neither Whirlwind nor Eaton tried to coach Gibson, but they frequently offered her tips on how to be a lady off the court. They taught her proper rules of etiquette and treated her like a family member, subject to the same rules of conduct and privileges as the doctors' children.

At the end of each school year in Wilmington, Gibson went to Lynchburg to live with Whirlwind and his family. Beginning in July 1947, Gibson, Whirlwind, Robert Jr. and a few others spent the summer traveling the ATA circuit. They played in Washington, D.C.; Philadelphia; New York; New Jersey; and Kentucky. With the chance to practice and play nearly every day during the summers, Althea, who was five feet eleven inches tall, developed a strong serve-and-volley game. She had a powerful serve and nearly always dominated the net with slashing volleys. In her first year traveling the ATA circuit, she won nine consecutive singles titles, including the ATA women's nationals. Her 6-3, 6-0 victory against Nana Davis in the final was the first of her still unequalled 10 consecutive ATA National titles.

In his role as surrogate father and mentor, Whirlwind had good reason to be proud of Gibson's performances. He found her efforts to be even more pleasurable when he shared the court with her in mixed doubles competition. Gibson and Whirlwind, who was over 45 when they first became a doubles tandem, won numerous ATA mixed doubles titles, including the ATA National crown seven times (1948-50, 1952-55). Their matches, which were nearly always dominated by Gibson, became must-see events for youngsters as well as senior players.

Said Jake Wells, an ATA official with the Mall Tennis Club in Washington, D.C., "My partner, Toni Williams, and I played them in the Mall tournament in Washington back in 1948. They beat us 6-1, 6-1. Althea did all the playing. Doc just stood at the net and stopped everything that was hit straight at him. You had to play him because Althea was just too strong. He played close to the net, the way the women in most mixed double matches play. He sure didn't get in Althea's way."

Gibson began her reign as the premier black woman tennis player in the country the same year Jackie Robinson broke the color barrier in major league baseball and Joe Louis completed his 10th year as the undisputed world heavyweight boxing champion. Blacks were on the move in the world of sports and some believed tennis soon would recognize its talented black stars.

In 1948, George Stewart, a left-hander who hit lethal topspin ground strokes from either side, became the first black to play in the NCAA tennis championships. Stewart earned the distinction while playing for South Carolina State. Dr. Reginald Weir, a former ATA champion, was the first black to play in the USLTA's National Indoor Championships.

"One has to keep in mind that Althea had to overcome the difficulty of not having the capacity to play against competition that would sharpen her game because she couldn't play at the country clubs where the best white players were," Dinkins said. "It was through sheer grit—and help of a few people—that she was able to get into some of those tournaments. Of course, once in, she demonstrated that she had the capacity to beat anybody."

ATA officials at the time quietly lobbied for Althea to break the color barrier at the U.S. Nationals, held each year at the West Side Tennis Club in Forest Hills, New York. USLTA officials responded to the ATA's efforts by contending that Althea was ineligible to play in the Nationals because she hadn't participated in a sufficient number of USLTA tournaments. ATA officials countered, saying she didn't play in those events because her applications were not accepted. It was the

USLTA's Catch-22, the cloak of dishonesty used to shield its policy of racial bigotry.

Alice Marble, the USLTA's top woman player of the 1930s, removed their cloak in an article published in the July 1950 issue of *American Lawn Tennis* magazine. Gibson first met Marble when the smooth-stroking Californian helped put another dent in the racial barriers by playing an exhibition against Mary Hardwick, England's No. 1 player, at the Cosmopolitan Club in 1944. After the exhibition, Hardwick teamed with Frances Gittens of the ATA and Marble played with the ATA's Lillian Van Buren for an exhibition doubles match. Gibson, then 14, was impressed by Marble's attacking style of play. Years later, Gibson's admiration for the four-time U.S. Nationals champion became boundless after Marble tongue-lashed the USLTA for barring Althea from the event. Marble wrote:

If tennis is a game for ladies and gentlemen, it's also time we acted a little like gentle people and less like sanctimonious hypocrites. If there is anything left in the name of sportsmanship, it's more than time to display what it means to us. If Althea Gibson represents a challenge to the present crop of women players, it's only fair that they should meet that challenge on the courts where tennis is played. I know these girls and I can't think of one who would refuse to meet Miss Gibson in competition. She might be soundly beaten for a while, but she has a much better chance on the courts than in the inner sanctum of the USLTA committee, where a different kind of game is played. If she is refused a chance to succeed or fail, then there is an un-eradicable mark against a game to which I have devoted most of my life and I would be bitterly ashamed.

The entrance of Negroes into national tennis is as inevitable as it has proven to be in baseball, in football and boxing; there is no denying so much talent. Speaking for myself, I will be glad to help Althea Gibson in any way I can. If I can improve her game or merely give her the benefit of my own experiences, as I have many other young players, I'll do that. If I can give her an iota more of confidence by rooting my heart out from the gallery, she can take my word for it: I'll be there.

Soon after Marble's editorial appeared, doors long closed cracked open. The Orange Lawn Tennis Association in South Orange, New

Jersey, accepted Gibson's entry for the Eastern Grass Court Championships, where she lost in the second round. Soon afterwards, she played in the National Clay Court Championships in Chicago, where Doris Hart defeated her in the quarterfinals.

Gibson's big league breakthrough was made without fanfare, a week before the U.S. Nationals. She would be among the 49 women competing for the USLTA National women's crown at the West Side Tennis Club in Forest Hills, the same club which earlier that year had barred Nobel Prize winner Dr. Ralph Bunche and his son from membership because of their color.

Wielding her racket like a lethal weapon, Gibson made an impressive debut at the U.S. Nationals, defeating Barbara Knapp in the first round. No. 3 seed A. Louise Brough cut short Gibson's stay at the West Side Tennis Club, outlasting Althea 6-1, 3-6, 9-7 in the second round. Gibson led 7-6 in the final set and seemed on the verge of scoring a major upset when a violent thunderstorm halted play.

"I'll never forget that storm," said Bertram Baker, the ATA's executive secretary and leader of the negotiating team that had pushed for Althea's long-delayed acceptance at the Nationals. "Fans were shouting from the stands for Althea's opponent to 'beat the nigger, beat the nigger.' I'll always remember it as the day the gods got angry. A flash of lightning came and knocked down one of the statues of the eagles on the stadium court." The next day, Gibson, still flustered by the storm and crowd reaction, lost the final three games.

With the doors finally flung open, Gibson began her climb to the top. She took lessons from black pro Sydney Llewelyn of New York, who changed her grip and instilled within her an I-can't-be-beat attitude. She became the first black to win a Grand Slam tournament title in 1956, defeating Great Britain's Angela Mortimer 6-0, 12-10 in the final of the French Championships. She won Wimbledon and the U.S. Nationals in 1957-58 and received the Associated Press and Babe Zaharias awards for being Woman Athlete of the Year each of those years. She also received a New York ticker-tape parade in July 1957 after becoming the first black to win Wimbledon.

"I told her to do it again just to show them that the first time wasn't a fluke," Llewellyn said.

AIDING ALTHEA

Tennis legend Billie Jean King was 13, growing up in southern California when she got her first glimpse of Gibson's powerful serve-and-volley game. "She had great presence and I could tell that the other women were intimidated by her," King said. "With her wingspan, power and shot production, she was awesome. She mixed power and spin and had great placement. She seemed to glide on the court. She had a big serve and in those days, you had to keep one foot on the ground when you served. Today's players don't realize that."

Dr. Robert M. Screen, Hampton University's tennis coach, often practiced with Gibson at ATA events when he was a junior player. "She was ahead of her time, especially with her kick serve, which jumped over your head if you didn't catch it on the rise," Screen says. "And she always hit a deep first volley when she followed her serve to the net. Her ground strokes were hit with whip-like action and she had a very nice slice backhand, which she said she copied from Ken Rosewall."

Despite her status as the game's premier player, Gibson felt unwelcome at many USLTA events and no one ever offered her a job that would allow her to continue her amateur tennis career. She was forced into early retirement as a tennis player after winning the 1958 U.S. Nationals.

"It was nice being the queen of tennis, but you can't eat a crown," Gibson said.

Empathizing with Gibson's experiences, King said, "It was a different era when she played. Some tournament directors cancelled their events because she was going to enter. It's hard for people today to imagine what she had to go through then. I'm very thankful for everything she's done."

For the next 30 years, Gibson, also a singer, struggled to find her niche. She recorded an album for Dot Records; got a bit part in a 1959 John Wayne movie, *The Horse Soldiers;* played tennis exhibitions as a warm-up act on the Harlem Globetrotters world tour; spent a few years on the women's professional golf tour and worked for more than 15 years in public relations-type positions in New Jersey. She was state athletic commissioner 1975-77.

In the early 1990s, Gibson lost her job with the New Jersey Governor's Commission on Physical Fitness due to cutbacks. Depressed and nearly broke, she suffered a stroke soon afterward and lived as a recluse until she died September 28, 2003. Fran Gray, her caretaker; tennis legend King; former pro Zina Garrison; and Angela Buxton, Gibson's Wimbledon doubles partner, were among only a few she allowed to visit her East Orange, New Jersey, home.

On the day Gibson died, King said, "We all know people who influence us, and if we are lucky, we meet a few in our lives who improve us. Althea Gibson improved my life and the lives of countless others. She was the first to break so many barriers, and from the first time I saw her play, when I was 13 years old, she became and remained one of my true heroines. It was an inspiration for me to watch her overcome adversity. Althea did a lot for people in tennis, but she did even more for people in general."

Garrison, the 1990 Wimbledon runner-up who reached a career high No. 4 in the world, visited Gibson at her home weeks before her death. "Knowing what Althea had done allowed me to believe that as a player I could do whatever I wanted to do," Garrison said. "Venus and Serena Williams are able to make their mark because the times have changed."

Venus, who like Gibson won back-to-back Wimbledon (2000-2001) and U.S. Open (2000-01) titles, said, "It would be foolish to forget Althea."

Though her career was short, Gibson's impact as a pioneer continues to loom large. "Politically, Althea's acceptance was crucial to my own," Ashe once said. "It made it easier for other blacks to follow."

The Williams sisters, Garrison, Lori McNeil, Chanda Rubin and Leslie Allen are among about a dozen black women who have followed Gibson on the women's pro circuit.

"It's so important that stories like Althea's be told so that folks will appreciate her accomplishments and those of others like her," Dinkins said. "Youngsters need to understand that nobody gets anywhere alone. Everybody stands on somebody else's shoulders, and all the African-American players who came after her, including the Williams sisters, stood on her shoulders. When any black achieves in any discipline, it helps everybody else. It's unfortunate that she never realized and reaped the rewards that she was due."

Gibson repeatedly said that it would be foolish for her to forget the importance of the shoulders offered by Dr. Johnson and Dr. Eaton during her climb to the top. After winning her first Wimbledon title in 1957, she sent telegrams to both of them. In her message to Whirlwind, she wrote, "Your faith, belief and encouragement helped tremendously. This victory is partly yours."

At the Wimbledon ball that night, she paid tribute to both doctors saying, "I remember particularly Dr. Robert W. Johnson and Dr. Hubert A. Eaton. It was in Dr. Eaton's home while completing high school that I received love and encouragement. It was through Dr. Johnson's efforts and assistance that I was able to travel all over the United States and gain much needed experience."

Gibson dedicated her first book, *I Always Wanted to Be Somebody,* to her two benefactors.

11

The Good Life

IN THE SAME WEEK that Althea Gibson won Wimbledon in 1957, Whirlwind appeared in local papers holding a headline announcing Althea's major triumph. His role in her development made him an even greater personality in the Lynchburg community.

Actually, Whirlwind was one of the town's most prominent personalities—black or white—years before Althea emerged as a superstar. Following in his father's footsteps, Whirlwind became a rarity in the segregated South: a black man with money and limited power. Like Papa Jerry, he owned the largest home in his neighborhood. Like Papa Jerry, he dabbled in real estate, owning several valuable properties, including the Happy Land Lake Club, a members' only restaurant just outside the city limits. Like Papa Jerry, he earned more money than any other black resident and was among the most respected members of his community.

The Johnson family enjoyed an idyllic existence during the early years in Lynchburg. Whirlwind thrived as the hard-working doctor; Peggy blossomed as the faithful, supportive wife.

"Peggy was a good wife, who also tried to be a good mother to her stepson, Bobby Jr.," said Hattie Robinson, who lived with the Johnsons in 1933, their first year of marriage. "I remember one time—I think Bobby Jr. was about seven at the time—she called him in the house and said, 'Now Bobby, I want you to sit down here and write your own mother a letter.' And she stayed with him until he finished. She and Dr. Johnson were very friendly, very pleasant together. They had not been married too long when I knew them."

THE GOOD LIFE

Inevitably, Whirlwind's love of tennis caused the first chill in the early years of the couple's marriage; later, his love of women led to its demise.

Determined to improve his game, Whirlwind began to spend most of his leisure time playing tennis at ATA events or on his backyard court. Agnes Lawson of Prairie View and Bennie Sides of Chicago were among many black players invited to train at Whirlwind's home and travel with him during the summer at his expense. His willingness to share his home and good fortune with others was one of his most endearing qualities.

Dr. Eaton said: "The thing that impressed me most about Whirlwind was that I could have called him and said, 'I'm in a jam now. I want you to loan me $5,000 and I'll give it back to you in three months.' And if he had it, he would send it to me, with no papers or nothing. If he was your friend, he would do anything for you. He was very free-hearted."

During most of the 1940s, Whirlwind's backyard court was the site of the ATA's annual Labor Day round-robin tournament. It was an invitational event, sponsored solely by Whirlwind, who invited the top ATA players, close friends and a few celebrities. Bobby Riggs and Frank Guernsy, top white players of the '40s, played an exhibition match there one year. Writer/photographer Gordon Parks Jr. also participated. The event was the ATA's most prestigious affair of that time.

"If you were invited to Lynchburg for Whirlwind's round robin, you were in," said Lucille Freeman of Washington, D.C. Two of her sons, Clyde and Harold, who were top ATA juniors in the '40s, often received invitations to play in the round robin. Whirlwind liked the Freeman brothers and believed they could be outstanding players. When Freeman's husband died, Whirlwind told her to send the boys to Lynchburg to live with him.

"I had no intentions of doing that," she said. Freeman said she felt a bit uncomfortable about her sons spending the summers in Lynchburg to be a part of what some Lynchburg residents described as a raunchy social scene.

"Whirlwind used to import some of the most beautiful women you ever saw from Cuba," said Sam Hutcherson, one of Whirlwind's regular tennis partners. "They were brought in to help entertain the players and other guests. There was always a lot of food, liquor and good times. He had some big poker games, too. I once saw Whirlwind bet $400 on a pair of tens. If white folks could have seen all the money them niggers had on the table they would have died. But you know, I liked going to Whirlwind's during the tournament because you got to see his basement. Man, being in that place was like dying and going to heaven."

When parties were in progress, Whirlwind's basement had the trappings and intimacy of an exclusive supper club. Red leather lounge chairs and couches were dispersed among rectangular columns that were encased in blue mirrors. The basement's centerpiece, however, was a decorative bar, which was always amply stocked with the best brands of liquor. Tennis trophies lined the shelves behind the bar. From a basement door, guests could climb stairs to the tennis court, passing through one of Whirlwind's prized possessions: a rose garden.

"His house was quite a socializing situation," said Dr. Helen Edmonds of Durham, North Carolina. "Prominent people from across the country in sports came there. His hospitality was unbounded. Everybody tried to gather there. Sometimes, he wouldn't have time to entertain them all. There was always good mirth, good conversation."

But these were not the best of times for Peggy, who, according to Whirlwind's friends and relatives, had become a problem drinker. The bottle had become the only way she could cope with Whirlwind's philandering ways and the realization that, though she truly loved him, they had very little in common.

Whirlwind was a gregarious, outgoing type. When he wasn't at work, he loved to travel and to mix with people. Peggy preferred to stay at home. He loved to hunt and fish; Peggy didn't. He loved attending football and basketball games, track meets and playing tennis; Peggy didn't. She helped him entertain during house parties, but stayed in the background. He was the smiling, gracious host; she was the quiet unassuming hostess.

Just as she and Whirlwind had formed a special friendship while he was still married to Annie, Peggy sensed that Whirlwind was forming what seemed to be similar friendships with other women. He had not really changed, but for Peggy, the circumstances had.

"Whirlwind was always fascinated by good-looking women and they found him to be fascinating," said Edmonds. "It never bothered him to have more than one woman with him in a social setting. But in my opinion, I don't think he ever thought of marrying any of them."

Edmonds met Whirlwind in 1934 when she was the dean of women at Virginia Seminary College. Though at times he seemed to view most women as sex objects, Edmonds and a few other smart and ambitious women were exceptions. He respected them and developed Platonic relationships with them. Edmonds lived in Lynchburg for only two years, but established a life-long friendship with the Johnson family.

Whirlwind rarely passed up an opportunity to test his charms on women. Tales of his exploits with women seem endless. At times, his dalliances produced more than complications and heartache.

In the late '30s, Whirlwind had an affair with a married woman. A baby girl was conceived. Whirlwind wanted to acknowledge publicly that he was the father, but the child's mother demanded his silence on the subject.

"I found out that I was his daughter when I was 17, getting ready to go to college," said Olivia (pseudonym) who resides in the Washington, D.C., area. "He paid for my college education, which I knew my parents couldn't afford. So I guess that's why my mother decided to tell me. Then he talked to me about it."

Olivia grew up believing Whirlwind was merely a close family friend. He took her hunting, bought her expensive clothes and taught her how to play tennis. "I was always forced to play tennis," she said. "He told me that he thought I could be another Althea Gibson. I used to ride with him to the tennis tournaments, but I never put it together that he was my father. Kids used to say it, but you know how vicious kids can be. My mother always denied it so strongly I never believed it. In a way, I wish I knew about it when I was younger. Then I could have been able to do more things, like join Jack and Jill (a black social club), things like that."

A year after Olivia was born, Peggy and Whirlwind adopted a baby girl, a decision that some of Whirlwind's relatives believed was made to shift his attention away from Olivia. The adopted baby, Carolyn Waltee, was the daughter of one of Whirlwind's nieces. Bobby Jr. said he was told that his parents adopted Carolyn to stabilize their relationship. The marriage, however, continued to deteriorate. In the early '40s, Peggy moved back to Thomaston, Georgia, her hometown.

Some say Peggy's drinking problem prompted her to return home; others say Whirlwind's decision to narrow his attention to Erdice Creasy-Rosser caused Peggy to return to Georgia. In the fall of 1933, Creasy-Rosser was injured in an automobile accident. A nerve in her left eye was paralyzed and her left hand was injured. Whirlwind treated her and grew to love her.

Erdice and Irving Rosser, who were married in 1930, were divorced seven years later. Whirlwind brought Erdice closer by finding positions for her to fill in his operations. In 1941, Erdice, who had resumed using Creasy, her maiden name, worked as Whirlwind's secretary at his country restaurant, the Happy Land Lake Club, the only nightclub for blacks in the area. A couple of years later, she moved into Whirlwind's office as his medical secretary. By then, she had become his most loyal and trusted employee and companion. Translation: she was his mistress.

In his personal life, Whirlwind followed the golden rule of the wealthy and powerful: do as I say, not as I do. He often lectured his female patients and young teenage girls about proper behavior, yet he frequently hosted parties where improper behavior was the rule, not the exception. He admonished his female patients not to be boisterous, not to smoke and not to get drunk under any circumstances, yet he condoned such behavior at his social gatherings. His double standards didn't go unnoticed. As he doled out the specifics of his moral code to his female patients, many gossiped about his wife being an alcoholic and his hedonistic personal life in general.

When Whirlwind and Peggy divorced in 1945, his pursuit of the good life continued. Materially, he had just about everything a black man could want, except, of course, the freedom of a white man. He spent the next decade fighting a system that measured a person's value strictly by the color of his skin. Whirlwind tried to open doors for blacks in medicine, politics and education, and he spent many hours in courthouses, seeking better housing for less fortunate blacks in his community.

He was driven, too, to remove the barriers that kept people of color away from tennis. He knew he could use his money to help do that. He focused more clearly on his goals after that 1950 stopover in Charlottesville, where he saw a sea of white boys playing tennis with the skill and poise that he yearned to possess. At 46, he knew he never would be able to reach the level of excellence of the white boys he saw in Charlottesville. But he saw no reason why black boys and girls, trained and coached properly, couldn't be as good. Whirlwind discontinued the round-robin ATA tournaments, realizing that "none of us who were playing in that were going anywhere in tennis."

Inspired by the white players he saw at the University of Virginia tennis courts, Whirlwind directed his money and energy into organizing and developing a program for black juniors. His goal simply was to find, coach and train black boys until one of them proved to be good enough to capture the interscholastic singles title in Charlottesville.

12

Junior Development

VICTOR MILLER AND ROOSEVELT MEGGINSON, the first blacks to play in the national interscholastic event in Charlottesville, gave less than stellar performances in their 1951 debuts. Neither won a game in first-round losses. Both caused Whirlwind to wonder if he could have been more helpful to them as a physician than he was as a coach. Their performances, Whirlwind declared, were exceedingly feeble.

Still, Whirlwind left Charlottesville proud to have helped topple another racial barrier. Tournament director Teddy Penzold promised that Whirlwind's players would be welcomed again the following year, which turned out to be a promising year for Whirlwind's then-infant junior development program. Whirlwind returned to the University of Virginia campus in the summer of 1952 with a squad that included a scrawny left-hander from Wilmington who oozed spark and fire.

Billy Winn made an impressive debut at the mostly white high school championship, displaying an assortment of forehand slices, chops and underpins. With no backhand and fast feet, Winn stunned James Ferrin of Phillips Exter High School 8-6, 4-6, 8-6 in the first round, and bounced Pete Pressinger of Hill High School in Potsdam, 6-3, 6-4 in the second round. Winn rested for less than a half hour when a local tournament official insisted that he play his third match of the day. Winn's opponent: Donald Dell, the tournament's No. 1 seed and national boys' champion. Dell, who received a first-round bye, had played only one match.

JUNIOR DEVELOPMENT

"*I played Billy Winn on the second tier of the back courts,*" said Dell, now an executive with SFX, a sports firm. "*He won the first set (6-1) so fast I didn't know what hit me. We were playing on a clay court and he slid and moved around easily. He was so damn quick. I was completely unprepared for him because I had never heard of him and never saw him play.*

"*He started making some errors in the second set, which I won 6-1, but it was a really tight match. Something struck me about him. He always gave me every benefit of doubt on line calls. If the ball I hit was close, he called it in. Years later, Arthur (Ashe) told me that Whirlwind taught all his players to give the point to the opponent if the ball was close.*"

Though Dell rallied to win the match, Whirlwind saw a shade of victory in Winn's defeat. The North Carolina youngster had won two tough matches in 90 degree heat and then had pressed the tournament's top player to the maximum before losing.

"Billy Winn was the fastest boy ever to play on the junior team," said Whirlwind, in an ATA annual program. "He was uncanny. He possessed good anticipation, learned quickly and was a very good competitor."

Winn had demonstrated to Whirlwind's satisfaction that creating a junior development program was a correct first step toward achieving his goal. The original concept for the junior program called for the best 10 interscholastic players to be trained for the entire summer of their selection. Several of Whirlwind's colleagues, including Dr. Eaton and Dr. C.W. Furlonge of Smithfield, North Carolina, volunteered their homes and courts to train two players each for a minimum of two weeks. Whirlwind took four players to train for the USLTA Interscholastic Championships.

"When we say train them, we were not interested in just changing their grips, etc.," Whirlwind said. "We intended to improve their game from a minor league status to a big league status. In the minors, a pitcher tries to throw a strike over the plate to reach the big leagues. A pitcher in the big leagues must throw for the corners. So our job was to teach the players how to serve to the corners and lines, instead of down the middle of the court. We wanted them to know the important points of each game to win and the most important games of each set to win. We also wanted to teach them court strategy and court ethics."

Winn was the program's first shining star. After spending the summer of 1953 training on Whirlwind's backyard court, Winn's game improved dramatically. Near the end of the summer, he surprised his hometown followers by defeating Julius "June Bug" Martin, also of Wilmington, at the ATA Nationals at Central State College in Wilberforce, Ohio. Martin, who was several years older than Winn, had defeated the rising junior star earlier that summer in straight sets. The victory gave Whirlwind something else to brag about.

"I believe that boys away from home will concentrate and develop quicker than if they stay in their own hometowns," Whirlwind said. "Proof of that contention is substantiated in the rapid development of Billy Winn, who in one year not only won the ATA National Interscholastic Championship, but also defeated the intercollegiate champion at the ATA Nationals."

Interest in tennis among blacks grew steadily during the time, but the pool of black athletes drawn to the game paled in comparison to the number of whites playing tournament tennis. Tennis lacked a following in black communities for two reasons:

- It was considered a game for wealthy whites, and
- It was considered a "sissy" sport, especially by the best young black athletes, who preferred team sports, such as basketball, baseball and football.

Unfortunately, very few of the black juniors who competed in ATA tournaments were willing to give up their summers to develop stronger games.

"We never had more than two boys during a year to be interested during those first few years," Whirlwind said. "The junior development committee was greatly disappointed in the reluctance of players to take advantage of this coaching."

The absence of interest among teenage blacks allowed Whirlwind to look for potential stars among the very young. In the spring of 1954, Whirlwind was introduced to a 10-year-old skinny kid from Richmond, Virginia, who already loved to play and was eager to improve. However, little Arthur Ashe Jr. didn't think anyone could know more about tennis than Ronald Charity, the man who taught him to play.

Charity, who was 19 when he attended Virginia Union University as a part-time student, taught tennis at Brooke Field Park, the city's black park. Ashe's father, Arthur Sr., was a special police officer in charge of the park. The Ashe family, Arthur Sr. and sons (Arthur Jr. and Johnnie), lived in a city-owned house inside the park, less than 20 yards from four tennis courts.

"I had a class of about 15 young people and Arthur, who was only seven, was a part of the class," Charity said. "The advantage he had was that he lived right there. So when I was out there during the early part of the day before the class got there, I would work with him, show him how to hit the ball and how to hold the racket."

Charity was among the ATA's top players when he met Whirlwind at an ATA tournament in Richmond.

"Actually, that was the first tournament I ever played in," Charity said. "Then I started going to all the tournaments. Dr. Johnson knew I wanted to improve my game; so he invited me to Lynchburg. I used to go there and play with his son, Bobby Jr."

Charity visited Whirlwind's home quite frequently each summer and joined Whirlwind and friends on several trips to ATA events. He remembered going to the ATA Nationals in Daytona Beach, Florida, with Whirlwind, Bobby Jr. and Althea Gibson in 1951.

On Charity's frequent early morning visits to Lynchburg, Bobby Jr. said, "I used to get up around seven on Saturday mornings and Charity would be sitting on the back porch waiting for me to come out. That meant he must have left his home in Richmond around 4:30 A.M. Then we'd play tennis all day, and afterward, he'd drive back to Richmond."

Charity often returned from Lynchburg convinced that he was a stronger player, as well as teacher. Charity's youngest pupil, Ashe, certainly believed that no one else had more tennis knowledge than Charity. After a summer of lessons from his tennis guru, Ashe, then eight, played in his first tournament and showed talent and promise. He lost to an older boy, but showed tenacity and desire. Charity took him to other local events and Ashe began to win.

"At 11, he'd reached the point where he needed more tournament experience," Charity said. "I couldn't take him because I was in school. So one day, when I was in Lynchburg, I told Dr. Johnson I had a little guy that I wanted him to take a look at. He said, 'Sure, bring him on up.'

"So, one afternoon, I took Arthur up to Lynchburg and let him hit some. Dr. Johnson said, 'He's not bad.' After we got back to Richmond, I continued to talk to Dr. Johnson about Ashe going up there to be a part of the junior development team. I had already talked to Ashe's daddy and he said that he wouldn't mind Arthur going up there to learn how to play if it's okay with Dr. Johnson. So Dr. Johnson finally agreed to take him."

Ashe spent only two weeks at Whirlwind's house during that first summer, but that was long enough for Ashe and Bobby Jr. to bump heads. Bobby Jr. was 26 when he was discharged from the Army in 1952. He and his new bride, Nerissa Lange, lived in an apartment in the same building where Whirlwind had his office.

They assisted Whirlwind with the junior development program. "From 7 a.m. to 7 p.m., the tennis players were the most important people in that house," Lange said. "My role was to be one of the helpers, to feed and help keep the place clean. Doc's role was to stay at the office and make the money. Bobby's role was to coach."

Bobby Jr.'s first coaching session with Ashe was exasperating at best.

"I tried to change his grip, but Arthur said, 'Mr. Charity taught me to hit it this way.' And he wouldn't change. I told him 'Mr. Charity's not teaching you now, I am.' I was a frustrated player who had been pushed into the coaching role; so I wasn't taking any shit."

Ashe's father was summoned to Lynchburg to intercede in the dispute. Like Whirlwind, Arthur Ashe Sr. was a strict disciplinarian who never tolerated defiance in his children or anyone else's. He told Arthur to do whatever Dr. Johnson or Bobby Jr. told him to do. Then he climbed back into his blue Ford and went back to Richmond. Problem solved.

"I never disobeyed my father," Ashe said.

Ironically, it was a time in history when disobedience in the pursuit of true freedom was not considered a vice. The U.S. Supreme Court reversed decisions that many people now say were immoral as well as illegal. In 1954, the nation's highest court declared that "separate but equal" educational facilities were inherently unequal and that segregation was therefore unconstitutional. Several years earlier, the Court had ruled that discrimination on interstate public transportation was illegal.

Throughout the South, the usually subservient black citizens shook the tranquility of their cities through protests and demonstrations. Many blacks died trying to ensure a better life for their children. The most effective black leaders during that time were clergymen and doctors, men who did not have to rely on whites for their livelihoods. Though soft-spoken and seemingly nonassertive, Whirlwind became the city's most important black leader. In July 1952, he accused the Lynchburg City Council of failing to correct slum conditions and of providing inadequate school facilities for blacks.

In a prepared statement published in the local paper, Whirlwind noted that while the Council had been studying the Baltimore plan for substandard housing improvements, other Virginia cities had built new low rent federal housing projects. The Council, he said, owed the people an explanation. He noted further that the Council was building "the fourth-best high school in the USA for white Lynchburg students . . . but this Council could be labeled a do-nothing Council for Negroes. Although all Negro facilities were neglected and in more need of repair than the white facilities, Council has done nothing to relieve them."

Whirlwind's public protest led to the construction of Lynchburg's first low rent housing project and the city's black schools received the financial aid needed to make improvements.

In October 1953, Whirlwind exposed a scheme Southern Railway was using in an attempt to keep blacks from riding on the trains in the same coaches with white passengers. In a newspaper story, he explained how he had tried to get tickets on a train going north, but was told there were no seats available. He asked a white friend to try to get the tickets for him and the friend was able to do so. In a letter addressed to the general passenger traffic manager for Southern, Whirlwind wrote, "It was my impression that the Supreme Court had made discrimination in interstate transportation illegal. If this is true, you will do the colored people in this city a great favor by informing your local agent and thereby avoid the possibility of legal action."

Whirlwind's reputation as a hard-working physician, who treated every patient with respect, regardless of his or her financial status, already had established him as a hero among blacks. But when he took it upon himself to spearhead the drive to fight racial prejudice, fully aware that he might be subjected to the wrath of the white establishment, respect turned to adulation.

"He faced every issue head-on," said Pauline Wheaton Maloney, who was the assistant principal at all-black Dunbar High School in the 1950s. "He was courageously independent and the backbone of his community."

M.W. Thornhill, owner of the Community Funeral Home in Lynchburg made this observation: "He would have been considered a radical (today). You know he had to be a super nigger, otherwise he would not have been able to do and say the things he did."

Another example of Whirlwind's "super nigger" boldness occurred when Mama Nancy, who was ailing, needed hospital care.

"Our mother suffered from asthma," Eva said. "She suffered so bad that in her later years, she spent the winters in Lynchburg with Robert or in New York with my sister, Elaine. The altitude was much higher there than it was in Plymouth and she didn't suffer as much. Each summer, she would come home."

Mama Nancy's condition worsened in the fall of 1954. Whirlwind sent an ambulance to Plymouth that took her directly to the Lynchburg General Hospital. Blacks at that time were not allowed to enter the hospital through the front door. They used a side door. But when Mama Nancy arrived in the ambulance, Whirlwind put her in a wheelchair and rolled her through the front door. Some hospital officials protested, but no one tried to stop him. After a brief hospital stay, Mama Nancy lived with Whirlwind. She never improved and died, at age 74, in early December 1954.

Neither civic duty nor family demands kept Whirlwind from his tennis mission, which had become twofold: to find a junior strong enough to win the USLTA Interscholastic title and to rest his mind from the mental weariness caused by his workload. His time spent with Ashe was often encouraging. Though only 10, Ashe won 12-and-under ATA events in Durham and Washington. What's more, the slender junior from

JUNIOR DEVELOPMENT

Richmond had discovered an exciting world of new friends and places. Ashe, who had never dreamed there were so many other black tennis players in the world, met black juniors from Ohio, Michigan, New York, Maryland and New Jersey. He returned to Richmond anxious for the year to pass so that he could return to this fantasy-like world that Whirlwind had thrown before him. Ashe believed the following summer would be just as exciting.

But in the summer of 1955, a 15-year-old black player from Los Angeles, California, joined Whirlwind's program and became an immediate sensation. Ashe was shoved into the background. Deep inside, Whirlwind believed that the Californian would be the player who would fulfill his dream. Ashe, who later would call Willis Fennell the most incredible player he'd ever seen, fully agreed.

13

The California Kid

As a hunter or a civil rights leader, Whirlwind never used a shotgun when a .22-caliber would suffice. For the most part, his strategy to overcome various racial obstacles was governed by homegrown logic laced with parental-instilled determination. The tactics he used to circumvent racism in tennis were more restrained, though doused with the same source of determination.

"He was not the kind of person who would do a lot of threatening or try to accomplish things by being belligerent," Eaton said. "When he was trying to get one of his boys in an all-white tournament, he'd find out who the tournament chairman was and simply talk to him. He'd say, 'Well, you know I got a boy here; he's a good boy and he's a good tennis player. You ought to let him play in this tournament.'"

Whirlwind often wrote letters to USLTA officials, to request applications for one of his juniors, information on the logistics of running a tournament or to complain about his players not being allowed to enter certain tournaments because of discriminatory actions. Once his players were accepted, he'd put on his public relations hat and spread the good word. He provided results and feature material on his players to black and white newspapers. He wrote articles about each of his players and took pictures of them with their white opponents. He edited and published newsletters and magazines so that others might know about the ATA junior development program.

Billy Winn's first-round victories in 1952-53 offered Whirlwind the first real hope of achieving his improbable dream of having a black player claim the USLTA Interscholastic title. A couple of years later, a young Californian named Willis Fennell had Whirlwind believing that his dream would be realized sooner rather than later.

Whirlwind and Bobby Jr. first saw Fennell play in Daytona Beach, Florida, at the ATA National Championships, where he won the boys 15-and-under title without losing a set. "He was the most fantastic 14-year-old I'd ever seen," Bobby Jr. said. "He was phenomenal; a young black Pancho Gonzalez. The following year, my father persuaded his mother to let him play with the junior development team."

Fennell, who grew up playing tennis on fast surfaces, developed a serve-and-volley game. Quick and agile, Fennell followed nearly every serve to the net and frequently slapped forehand or backhand volley winners past his opponents. With Hall of Famer Pancho Gonzalez providing some coaching tips, Fennell became a smooth-stroking, untouchable tennis machine. Blacks were allowed to play in USLTA tournaments in California, and Fennell finished the 1954 season as the state's No. 1 ranked player in the 14-and-under category. ATA officials believed Fennell had the talent and heart needed to be a top player in U.S. tennis, if not the world.

Fennell was 15 when he played at the 1955 USLTA Interscholastic Championships, after Richard Malloy of Hillside High School in Durham, North Carolina, declined the invitation. Malloy qualified for the bid by capturing the ATA Interscholastic title, defeating Henry Livas of Phenix High School in Hampton, Virginia, in the final. Whirlwind immediately selected Fennell to join Livas for the trip to Charlottesville. Fennell beat Walt Straley of London High in Bethesda, Maryland, 8-6, 6-2 and Livas lost to Al Roberts of New York 6-1, 6-2 in the first round in Charlottesville. Top seed Crawford Henry, the nation's No. 9 ranked junior, beat Fennell 6-4, 6-3 in the second round. Believing that he would have Fennell competing for the Charlottesville title for the next three years, Whirlwind was thrilled by Fennell's performance and confidently predicted that if "he doesn't let success swell his head, Willis Fennell would be a future winner of the USLTA National Interscholastic Championship."

Still, Whirlwind believed that Fennell's temperament, more than his talent, would determine if his prediction would become reality. Fennell gave signals that he could be testy, at times defiant. Unlike Southern-bred blacks, Fennell was unfamiliar with feelings of inferiority that were brought on by law-enforced segregation of the races. Fennell had spent his formative years excelling in tennis against the country's very best white players. In his mind, he was free to be the best that he could be—or the worst that he could be.

Except for the automatic invitations offered to semifinalists of the ATA National Intercollegiate Championships, Whirlwind used his instincts and personal bias to determine other players to train at his Lynchburg home. In 1955, Whirlwind's junior development team consisted of only three players: Fennell, Livas and Beverly Coleman, also from Los Angeles, California. The team practiced on Whirlwind's court during the week and traveled together each weekend to local ATA tournaments. Wherever they played, Fennell always routinely beat Livas in the boys' 18-and-under final and always won the boys' 15 event as well.

Livas liked Fennell as a traveling companion and teammate, but hated to see him across the net in tournament competition. Though he was two years older than Fennell, Livas, Virginia's black high school junior champion, felt like a beginner whenever he went up against the speedy Californian's attacking style of play.

"I just got tired of losing to Fennell every week," Livas said. "So I packed my bags and went home. Doc wasn't too pissed off at me. I think he understood."

Fennell's emergence as an ATA junior superstar prompted Whirlwind to think younger. Instead of focusing just on high school-aged players, he began inviting 12-year-olds to join his program. He didn't have to look very far for his first young candidate. The day after Livas left, Whirlwind called Richmond to let little Arthur Ashe know that his room was ready.

Livas didn't elude embarrassing moments against Fennell by leaving Lynchburg. Later that summer, he clashed for the final time with Fennell in the ATA National Junior final in Durham, North Carolina. Fennell prevailed 6-1, 6-2. Fennell also beat Ashe in the boys' 15-and-under category 6-2, 6-1. Ashe, however, showed his potential by beating Willis Thomas of Washington, D.C., in the ATA National boys' 12-and-under final 6-3, 6-4.

Convinced that Fennell was strong enough to compete against the best black men players, Whirlwind entered Fennell in the ATA men's singles championships, which was held the following week in Wilberforce, Ohio. Many ATA officials and top-ranked players shared Whirlwind's optimism about his mercurial junior star. But instead of welcoming the challenge, several ATA top men's players, fearing that their title would be captured by a 15-year-old, quashed Fennell's hopes of being the youngest ATA men's champion by barring all juniors from competing in the men's division that year. Whirlwind was incensed by the decision, and Fennell vowed that he wouldn't play in any future ATA-sanctioned events. Fennell was livid about his exclusion from the men's event and became defiant and hostile toward the organization and its membership.

Some believed that the level of his arrogance rose with each USLTA title that he captured. Bobby Jr., who had the task of mentoring a player that he could neither beat nor control, explained what occurred the day Fennell left the junior development program.

"I was trying to coach Fennell by the book," Bobby Jr. said. "I would read the book one day, then the next day I would give the lesson. He was playing extremely well; so we sent him to a USLTA tournament in Wilmington, Delaware, and he won the boys' 16s and 18s without losing a set.

"After we returned, he was practicing his lob one day and I said, 'Come on, Willis, you've got to follow through to the spot no matter what stroke you're hitting. He got angry, slammed his racket down and, in essence, said, 'I quit.' My father called his mother, who begged him to stay, but he said, 'No, I've had it.' And that's the last I ever heard of him."

Ashe, who, at the time, viewed Fennell as a role model, said Fennell was more than a cut above the rest of the black players. Years later, Ashe would say, "I was in awe of Willis Fennell."

Whirlwind considered Fennell's departure a serious setback. He believed Fennell had the ability, desire and competitive spirit, but not the temperament needed to be a national tennis champion. Whirlwind realized that in order for a black to smoothly circumvent the racial roadblocks of that era, he would have to be properly packaged for success. He decided that Ashe and every other promising black junior would be groomed and indoctrinated to play a game within the game of tennis.

14

Lessons in Humility

Invitations to attend the junior development program were sent to the players' high school coaches with Whirlwind's ground rules and expectations clearly defined.

In the spring of 1955, Whirlwind directed Phenix High School coach Rufus Gant to ship Livas to Lynchburg immediately after the last day of school. "There will be no charge for room and board," Whirlwind wrote in a letter that Gant kept in a scrapbook. "They will be expected to keep the court and yard cleaned. They will study tennis and practice as directed."

The players also received lessons in humility, something Whirlwind considered as important to their development as mastering the forehand drive. The town's most outspoken civil rights activist indoctrinated his young guests with a variation of the turn-the-other-cheek philosophy that Brooklyn Dodgers general manager Branch Rickey urged Jackie Robinson to embrace in 1947, when Robinson integrated major league baseball.

Whirlwind wasn't content to have his team play in Charlottesville once a year. He intended to open the doors of every USLTA tournament within driving range of Lynchburg and some beyond. He anticipated resistance and rejections. He believed that if they were allowed to play at some country clubs, problems, perhaps violence, might mar the breakthrough. Segregation, after all, remained the operative word in the South. It was clear, too, that, for the most part, white America still wanted to believe in the inferiority of blacks.

While black leaders of that era urged their followers to use nonviolent tactics in their fight for true freedom, many white Southerners, some aided by local police, violently resisted black America's cry for justice. Reports of racial attacks made headlines in newspapers across the nation. History books overflow with examples of white America's unfairness and brutality toward blacks struggling for equality:

- In August 1955, Emmett Till, a 14-year-old from Chicago, was abducted by a group of white men while visiting his aunt in Money, Mississippi. Till's body, weighed down by a 150-pound cotton gin fan, was recovered a few days later from the bottom of the Tallahatchie River. He had been murdered for whistling at a white woman.
- In December 1955, Rosa Parks, an Alabama seamstress, was arrested for refusing to give up her seat to a white man on a Montgomery public bus. Her resistance led to a year-long boycott of public transportation in Montgomery. The boycott was led by a 27-year-old minister named Martin Luther King Jr.
- In February 1956, a federal court in Birmingham, Alabama, ordered the University of Alabama to admit its first black student, Autherine Lucy, who was harassed and later suspended and expelled by the University's trustees. The NAACP was outlawed in Alabama in May of 1956.
- In September 1957, three years after the Supreme Court had ruled school segregation to be unconstitutional, angry whites jeered Elizabeth Eckford, a 15-year-old black girl who was turned away from Central High School in Little Rock, Arkansas, by National Guardsmen with fixed bayonets. Eckford walked through a mob of about 500 white citizens, some of whom shouted slogans of hatred, such as "Lynch her, lynch her"; "No nigger bitch is going to get in our school"; and "Let's take care of the nigger."

Whirlwind realized that the genteel world of tennis might be equally dangerous and resistant to change. He didn't want to put his players in harm's way or to damage his program. So he demanded that his players display manners beyond reproach. For Whirlwind's players, court ethics meant more than extending common courtesy and sportsmanship. He preached subservience. He instructed them never to argue with the um-

LESSONS IN HUMILITY

pire, to pick up the balls after every odd game and give them to the opponent when changing sides. He insisted that balls hit close to the line be called in favor of the opponent, even if the call is incorrect. He told them that they must never argue with their opponents during a match.

"Dr. Johnson used to tell us when you hit a ball on the line and they call it out, hit it six inches inside the line," said New Yorker Bobby Davis, who was 15 when he joined Whirlwind's team in the late 1950s. "If they call it out again, hit it a foot inside the line."

Charles Brown of Durham recalled how Whirlwind curbed his habit of hurling his racket in disgust after bad shots or unfavorable rulings. "I was playing a tournament in Baltimore," Brown said. "After I won the first two sets, the officials said it was a best-of-five set match, not two-of-three. So I got mad and started throwing my racket. Doc walked out there and said, 'The next time you throw that racket, just go pack up everything and go home.' That was the last time I threw a racket. He wanted us to be disciplined emotionally, too."

Whirlwind's traveling team in the late '50s included some of the most gifted black juniors of that era. But two of his players, William Neilson and Horace 'Red' Cunningham, lacked the self-control and discipline that Whirlwind knew they would need to be racial pioneers. Neilson, a superb athlete, was the star player and captain of the football, basketball and tennis teams at Phenix High School in Hampton, Virginia. He won the black state high school singles title in 1956 and 1958 and the ATA National junior title in 1956. Instead of executing his household chores, the often-mischievous Neilson used to go behind the bar in Whirlwind's basement to enjoy a few scotch and sodas or high balls before noon. "Dr. J got suspicious; so he started measuring the bottles before leaving for work in the morning," Neilson said.

Cunningham, who attended Dunbar High in Lynchburg, won the black state high school title in 1957. Matches between Cunningham and Neilson were as memorable for their explosive outbursts as they were for their extraordinary shot making. Once, while being humiliated by Cunningham in a match in Hampton, Neilson, in frustration, hurled his racket on top of a three-story building next to the courts. He then calmly summoned Cunningham to the net and said, 'Red, excuse me for a minute while I climb up this motherfucking wall to get my racket.' "

Weeks later, Cunningham pulled a similar temper tantrum in Lynchburg while Neilson whipped him. Whirlwind once described this trouble-seeking duo, who were fair-skinned blacks, as "two peas in a pod who deserved each other."

In an analysis of Cunningham, Whirlwind said that he had "the best backhand in ATA tennis," but noted far more negatives than pluses in assessing Cunningham's potential. Wrote Whirlwind: "Has no concentration, no plans, slightly confused while playing and likes to volley while moving in. Has dangerous serve, but rarely uses it, too lazy. Is satisfied to reach the semifinals. Doesn't have a worry in the world. Likes to be seen and is often disturbing trying to attract attention. He is very provocative, evasive and positively doesn't like to work. Will wait until the very last minute to do anything you'd tell him to do."

Willis Thomas, a 15-year-old member of the junior development team when Cunningham was also on the squad, grinned when talking about Cunningham's often-obstinate behavior, giving a perfect example of what Whirlwind had written.

"Red's cleanup assignment at the house one day was to get the weeds out of Doc's rose garden," said Thomas. "But Red wouldn't do it. So when Doc got home from the office, he told Red that if the weeds weren't gone by tomorrow morning, he wasn't going to take Red on the next trip. Red just sat there acting cool. Didn't move a muscle. But that night, Red was down on all fours crawling in the rose garden with a flashlight, pulling up weeds. It was the funniest thing."

Cunningham thrived on his self-appointed role as the team's resident wit and court jester. "Once, I was traveling with the team—I believe we were in North Carolina somewhere—when we stopped along the road to get some ice cream at a little country store," said Erdice Creasy, who helped Whirlwind manage the junior program. "Red went up to the lady and asked for a cone of ice cream. She said, 'We don't serve colored here.' And Red said, 'That's okay, I don't want any colored ice cream, I want vanilla.'"

Whirlwind's son, Bobby Jr., believed a stable family environment might have helped Cunningham become a major figure in tennis. "Red was a tremendous talent," Bobby Jr. said. "I tried to get my father to adopt him. He had some serious social problems and I believe if my father had adopted him, he would have really gone places in tennis. For a while, he was the only player who could consistently beat Ashe."

Neilson also had his share of victories against Ashe, Whirlwind's rising 15-year-old star. The son of Herman, a Hampton Institute college professor, and Theodora, a high school teacher, Neilson puzzled Whirlwind with his immature behavior. In an evaluation of Neilson, Whirlwind noted: "Neilson is a much better tennis player than his record indicates. His biggest problem has been self-control. He has 'almost' won many matches and many championships. His best match was a defeat in Wilmington, Delaware, in the USLTA Delaware State Championship, where he went three sets and was cheated out of so many match points the tournament director changed officials."

Neilson's expletive-laced reaction to those bad calls cost him a spot on Whirlwind's traveling team. "Billy was really pissed," Thomas said. "He called those officials every kind of motherfucker he could think of." Whirlwind understood Neilson's anger, but couldn't tolerate that kind of outburst at an integrated tournament. He sent Neilson home and refused to invite him to any other integrated tournament, including the National Junior Championships in Kalamazoo, Michigan.

Whirlwind felt his players' pain when they were cheated or treated unfairly. Still, he pushed them to ignore the pain and unfairness. "We're going into a new world," Whirlwind would say to his players during pep talks. "We've got to be extra careful. We've got to turn the other cheek. All they want is an excuse to keep us out."

Ashe, Thomas and Bobby Davis, the younger members of Whirlwind's traveling team, were eager to please and never misbehaved. Charles Brown and Joe Williams, who were pre-teens when they learned to play tennis in Durham, North Carolina, felt privileged to be a part of such an elite group and rarely stepped out of line. They grew up in a slum area near the Algonquin Club and quickly became the club's best junior players.

"The club members took us to a tournament in Orangeburg, South Carolina, once," Brown said. "Joe and I could beat their kids; so I guess they figured it wouldn't be right not to train Joe and me."

Williams and Brown were Nos. 1 and 2 among black juniors in North Carolina. Brown won the 12-and-under state title and Williams won the 15-and-under crown. Williams, who also won the ATA National title in 1958, was an annual summer guest at Whirlwind's camp. Whirlwind brought him back to camp even after he no longer was eligible to compete as a junior.

"My father figured that he was good practice fodder," Bobby Jr. said.

Whirlwind loved Williams' fighting spirit and his willingness to carry his load around the house. "Joe is the kind of guy around the house that you don't have to tell to do things," Whirlwind said. "Outside or inside, he loves to work and makes his host or hostess happy to have him around."

Whirlwind's rules slowly began to pay dividends. In 1958, tournament officials at the USLTA National Interscholastic in Charlottesville asked him to bring five players to compete instead of the usual two. The next year, the junior development team was invited to stay overnight with the white players in a campus dormitory. The players were also invited to use other campus facilities, including the movie theatre.

"Strange happenings," Brown said. "We arrived late that first night. They assigned us to a dormitory that had about 15 other guys who were already there and asleep. When we woke up the next morning, we were the only ones there. They had moved their beds out. Also, they gave all the players passes to go to the theatre, but we had to sit upstairs. Strange."

In the late 1950s, Whirlwind's junior program members captured nearly every junior title available at ATA events. They also won several USLTA junior tournaments, though they weren't always given warm welcomes or fond farewells.

"We played an integrated tournament in Maryland—I believe it was the Maryland State Championships," Brown said. "The final was between Joe Williams and Arthur Ashe. The tournament officials came out that morning and left the trophies. They didn't bother to stay and present them."

Davis said the team received a more disturbing welcome from USLTA officials in the Midwest. "Ashe, Doc and I were traveling together to an integrated tournament in Ohio," Davis said. "The officials had confirmed by phone that our entry had been received and that we were in the draw. When we arrived, they took one look at us and told us we were not in the draw. Had it not been for the fact that we were

LESSONS IN HUMILITY

going to the junior nationals in Kalamazoo, Michigan, anyway, we would have driven from Virginia to Ohio for nothing."

Whirlwind accepted racial slights as part of the price that had to be paid for meaningful progress. He urged his players to do the same. "I've seen too many Negroes wreck their lives through hatred of whites," Whirlwind said. His players during those pioneering days admired the soft-spoken physician for the many sacrifices—both financial and personal—that he made in their behalf. They watched him show a similar level of generosity toward his neighbors and friends. And they respected him for helping others to overcome the racial barriers, which they knew stifled their growth and development as human beings, as well as tennis players.

Many of the black juniors who lived and trained at his home during the late '50s, verbalized their affection for Whirlwind with another nickname. They called him Dr. J.

"You've got to give Dr. J credit," said Thomas, Ashe's doubles partner in the 12-and-under and 14-and-under divisions. "He was always polite and courteous to white officials, but I never felt that he feared them. He was determined to make a difference."

Indeed, Whirlwind never hesitated to publicly condemn USLTA officials who showed their racial bias by refusing to accept entries from qualified black players, as he did in this letter to a junior tournament director:

```
              AMERICAN TENNIS ASSOCIATION
        Dr. R. Walter Johnson, First Vice-President
           Chairman, Interscholastic Committee
                    1001 Fifth Street
                   Lynchburg, Virginia

                                             July 10, 1959
Mr. William F. Riordau
Fashion Shop
Salisbury, Maryland

Dear Mr. Riordau:
   I received your letter today written July 7, in which you in-
form me,
         "The entries for the Middle Atlantic, which
         starts at the Congressional Country Club in
         Washington on Wednesday, July 8th, closed July
         3rd. The draw was completed on Sunday, July
         5th."
```

Whirlwind used the dinner meal to remind his juniors of the importance of being well-groomed gentlemen at all times, but especially while playing at white tournaments. He taught them how to use each piece of silverware during meals, warned them not to talk while chewing food and instructed them to always say "yes sir" and "no sir" to adults.

In a 1960 report to the ATA leadership, Whirlwind proudly boasted of his team's achievements against other ATA juniors and its integration of several USLTA junior events. "Juniors in our development program, to my knowledge, have never lost a junior match to a junior not on our team and have, in most instances, invaded men's singles with success," Whirlwind said. "We have played all over the East and some Central states, opened up many tournaments to Negroes. The number of tournaments we have played in for the first time reads like a 'Who's Who in Tennis.'"

But once his players began earning headlines in newspapers across the country, other ATA officials wanted a share of the limelight. Whirlwind resisted their overtures, which he considered too little, too late.

From its beginning in 1951, the junior development program was an idea that Whirlwind created and nurtured almost single-handedly. Indeed, in the early years, it was a plan that he alone believed would one day be useful and productive. Against strong opposition, Whirlwind organized and supervised the ATA's first separate junior national championships, which were held in 1955. He noted that the USLTA held a separate junior event in Kalamazoo and shared USLTA officials' philosophy that having a separate event for juniors made it more prestigious, albeit more expensive. He solicited donations from college buddies and ATA members, but most of the money to feed, clothe and develop these youngsters came out of his own pocket. He resented the Johnny-come-lately mentality of some ATA officials, who ignored him and the program during the early years. And he was especially critical of Bertram Baker, the ATA's executive secretary, who seemingly opposed most of Whirlwind's ideas.

"The success of our program has been made without the blessings of the Administration," Whirlwind wrote in the 1960 ATA souvenir program.

15

A Divisive Feud

WHETHER HE WAS TREATING a patient or trying to charm a recalcitrant USLTA official on the logic or fairness of allowing his black juniors to play an event, Whirlwind always spoke calmly and with palpable confidence. Rarely did he show anger or dismay, except, of course, when the subject of a conversation involved New York-based Bertram Baker, the man Whirlwind nicknamed "The Boss."

A bitter feud and power struggle developed between Whirlwind, the ATA's first vice president, and Baker, the organization's executive secretary. Dr. Sylvester Smith, also of New York, was the ATA's president, but Baker held the power. The feud began when Whirlwind, following the example of the USLTA, organized a separate national event for juniors. "We incurred the wrath of The Boss because of that," Whirlwind said.

Despite Baker's rejection of the idea and refusal to provide financial support, the separate junior event proved successful. Whirlwind believed the separate event helped strengthen his junior development program, which had begun to draw rave reviews from the media.

"The success of this program has been costly," Whirlwind once noted. "Personal friends have been lost, while others have suffered embarrassment. Although I take care of all of the players while in Lynchburg, Virginia, feed them and house them while there, furnish laundry service and often have to purchase equipment, I have been accused of making money out of the program."

Following that accusation, which Whirlwind said was made by "an executive officer who doesn't pay a dime to the ATA," Whirlwind named John Wheeler, president of Mechanics & Farmers Bank (Durham, North Carolina), as the program's treasurer. Wheeler controlled the flow of funds and each year published names and amounts of all donations received.

By 1959, even Baker applauded Whirlwind for his work as director of the junior development program. But it was time, he said, for the program to be directed under the auspices of the organization, not Whirlwind.

"The ATA wanted to have identification with Dr. Johnson's program," said Wilbert Davis, who won his first of four ATA national singles titles in 1958. "They wanted it to have an ATA label and that created tension. Doc Johnson was an independent guy. He wasn't part of the Eastern block."

The internal fighting was divided along regional lines. Members of the "Eastern block" accused Whirlwind of stacking his program with Southern players. They called him a grandstander, accused him of stealing money from the program and attacked him vociferously at ATA meetings.

One former ATA president characterized the attacks as "a typical case of the Jesus Christ Syndrome. Anytime we as Negroes see one of our brothers doing well and being recognized in the media, we try to nail him to the cross."

Whirlwind retaliated through the media, his criticisms aimed mainly at The Boss. He once told a reporter that the ATA was in the hands of "powerful, vicious West Indians in New York." Baker, who was born on the Island of Nevis, British West Indies, was Whirlwind's obvious target. A longtime ATA member, Baker's career as a New York politician might have prepared him for his sometimes nasty, public squabble with Whirlwind.

In 1948, Baker became the first black elected to any public office in Brooklyn when he won a New York State Assembly seat. He was the majority whip of the Assembly in 1966-68 and served in the Assembly for 22 years. Involved in the ATA since its inception, Baker joined the Utopian Tennis Club in Brooklyn in 1916 and subsequently served as president and chairman of the board of directors. He was elected exec-

A DIVISIVE FEUD

utive secretary in 1936 and served in that capacity for 30 years. He played a key role in the negotiations that led to the USLTA's acceptance of Althea Gibson's application to become the first black to play in the U.S. Nationals at Forest Hills, New York, in 1950.

Two years later, he strengthened his status as the ATA's most powerful official by helping formulate the deal that gave ATA National champions automatic bids into the U.S. National Championship. More importantly, as the ATA's executive secretary, Baker determined which players besides the ATA champion would play in the prestigious USLTA event.

In 1952, George Stewart, then-reigning ATA champion and Dr. Reginald Weir, a former champion (1931-33, 1937), became the first black men to play at Forest Hills. Both lost in the first round. In 1954, Baker selected Dr. Eaton and Edgar Lee of Washington, D.C., to play at Forest Hills. Neither Eaton nor Lee was a former ATA National champion, and many believed Baker selected them because of friendship or for political reasons. Australian great Ken Rosewall soundly thrashed Lee, and Eaton played so poorly that Tony Trabert, U.S. National champion (1953-55) had trouble giving him a game. The final score: 6-0, 6-0, 6-1. From 1955 to 1957, Baker chose the same four players: Harold Freeman, Clyde Freeman, Wilbert Davis and Vernon Morgan. Only Clyde Freeman was not a New Yorker. Robert Ryland, 1955-56 ATA champion, also was selected in 1955, and George Stewart, a seven-time ATA National champion joined the foursome in 1957.

Whirlwind was incensed by Baker's refusal to give his promising juniors—Ashe, Cunningham and Williams—a chance to play the grass court event. Whirlwind said Baker promised to choose the young trio to play Forest Hills in 1959, but reneged on that promise, choosing only Ashe. He sent all three to New York weeks before the event and arranged for them to practice on grass a week before the event. "It was discovered that Cunningham, the best player at that time on grass, and Williams had been given a dirty deal by Mr. Baker, who had placed a New Yorker's name above theirs," Whirlwind said. "I know that the USLTA takes the names of the players from the top of Mr. Baker's list and the only way ATA players can play is to be recommended by Mr. Baker, who may send in 20 names. Williams has never been recommended. Cunningham once, Ashe once. Mr. Baker's antagonism for the junior development program prevents him from giving the juniors a chance to develop on grass."

Whirlwind campaigned for Baker's ouster. He wrote an open letter to the black-owned *New York Amsterdam News* calling for Baker to resign. Baker said he responded to Whirlwind by telling him where to go. On Whirlwind's charge that he was unfair to his junior players, Baker would only say, "We disagreed about some things, but Johnson felt because I disagreed with some of his opinions that I was opposed to him. That was not the case."

The clash of the ATA titans continued through the late '50s. As the organization's first vice president, Whirlwind was next in line to become president at the 1960 annual meeting. He knew, however, that Baker and his Eastern block, would vehemently oppose him as president. So Whirlwind made a wily move by seeking to install his chief comrade, Dr. Hubert Eaton, as president.

"Whirlwind was going to wrestle control of the ATA from these people who had carried it along for so many years," Eaton said. "He had several people there representing clubs. He even paid the club fees for one or two clubs so he could have as many votes as possible. He knew that he wasn't acceptable as president for several reasons, one being that when you make a switch like that—to put somebody out—generally, you're doing it to put yourself in and those who were in control of the ATA at that time didn't want Whirlwind."

Whirlwind told Eaton that he would stop fighting and that he would instruct his block of supporters to vote for Eaton.

"I told him I don't want it; I'm too busy at home," Eaton said. "Then he went to Sylvester Smith and told him that if he withdrew his name as president, he would support Dr. Eaton. Syl said he would. Bertram Baker said that it was fine and so did all the other ATA leaders. So I found myself with all the support to be president and that's how I became president."

With Ashe and his other juniors on the rise, Whirlwind figured Eaton would be an ally in his bid to get his junior program additional support. His battles with Baker caused deep wounds, rattled his confidence and, in time, made him wonder if achieving his goal of showing that black juniors were capable of being great tennis champions was worth stirring up such animosity.

"I have been publicly insulted in meetings," Whirlwind said. "Not allowed to even speak at times, accused of working for self-aggrandizement, accused of trying to destroy the ATA. Persons in office who voted with me have been kicked out of office. I have been publicly accused of trying to buy the ATA votes. The quality of the play of our junior graduates and current juniors is all the reward I want for the time, effort and money spent. I can now lay me down to sleep and laugh up my sleeve at my accusers, who have been trying to keep the juniors down."

16

King Arthur

WHIRLWIND REFUSED TO ALLOW his squabble with Baker and other ATA leaders to distract him from achieving his goal of watching a black junior capture the USLTA Interscholastic singles title. By 1959, deep in his heart, he had come to believe that Ashe, the wiry youngster from Richmond, was on course to conquer Charlottesville.

During his early trips to Charlottesville, Whirlwind had learned that most of the top-ranked white teens had begun playing tennis as pre-teens and had excellent coaching throughout their development. In contrast, most of Whirlwind's players during those early years were late bloomers, good athletes who lacked the match toughness that comes with competing against stronger and more experienced players on a daily basis. Little Ashe was the exception.

The decision to invite 11-year-old Ashe into the program was an experiment in long-range planning. At the time, Whirlwind wasn't sure the scrawny, Southern-bred kid was the right candidate for the experiment. Ashe was sickly-thin and didn't look as if he was strong enough to withstand a stiff wind, much less smack a ball across the net with any pace. Little Ashe, however, proved to be a fighter with a big heart and boatloads of determination. In practice sessions, he threw his body into every shot and chased down every ball.

Except for that incident with Bobby Jr.—when Ashe initially refused to change his grip—neither Bobby Jr. nor Whirlwind ever had a problem with Ashe, who listened, watched and learned what to do to succeed on the court as well as off the court. He performed his daily chores without resistance and played each practice match as if it were a tournament final. "The one thing I noticed [was] that if you didn't win, you didn't stay in the program," Ashe said.

The daily drills were mandatory and the emphasis was on building consistency. Ashe became the camp's hardest worker and model student. He thrived on the regimentation and became the program's most consistent baseliner.

"We had to hit so many shots down the line, so many cross-court, then reverse it—cross-court and down the line," Ashe said. "We had daily contests to see who could hit the most forehands without making an error, the most forehand returns of serve, deep forehand shots, forehand approach shots and forehand passing shots. Then we ran through the whole series on the backhand."

Ashe, the first player on the court in the morning and the last to leave at night, loved every moment he spent on the court. He practiced as if he believed that perfection—though just out of reach—indeed was attainable.

"Arthur came to New York to practice when he was about 15, and all he'd want to do was drills," Bobby Davis said. "He could hit backhands for hours. I, for one, wanted to play sets. Arthur had so much self-control."

With consistency and tenacity, Ashe quickly established himself as the player to beat in his age group. Ashe dominated the 12-and-unders, and at 14, he was the top gun in the 16-and-unders. He won the 16-and-under ATA National titles in 1957-58 and was strong enough to beat most of the older juniors as well, except those in Whirlwind's program. Whirlwind's top guns—Joe Williams, 'Red' Cunningham and Billy Neilson—enjoyed practicing with Ashe, who was much smaller, because he was steady and would run down nearly every shot. They liked competing against him in tournaments because they knew that when a set or match was at stake, they could step up the pace and overpower him. Painful though they might have been, those early losses to Whirlwind's older and stronger juniors made Ashe mentally tougher and more determined to surpass them. One by one, Ashe moved ahead of Whirlwind's older top juniors.

WHIRLWIND

At 15, Ashe was still wiry, but finally strong enough to match the power of the ATA's top juniors. Playing for Richmond's Maggie Walker, he beat Cunningham 6-2, 6-2 in the final of the black state singles championships in 1959. Neilson needled Cunningham as he struggled against Ashe's laser-like ground strokes. Catching a glimpse of Neilson's smiling face, Cunningham shot back, "Now I know how you must have felt when I kicked your ass here last year, Billy."

Neilson, of course, had fallen to Ashe for the first time at an ATA event a year earlier.

"I was playing Ashe in a tournament in Norfolk," Neilson said. "Livas passed by the court with two girls and told me to hurry up; he had a date for me. I was leading Ashe 5-2 in the first set and yelled out, 'Don't go anywhere; I'll be through in a minute.' About an hour and a half later, I had lost the match. Never did beat Ashe again."

The next year, Ashe firmly established himself as the premier black junior by capturing the black state and national interscholastic titles. He defeated Phenix High's Doug Smith 6-4, 6-0 in the state final in Petersburg, Virginia, and long-time nemesis Joe Williams in the national final in Durham. "At the beginning of the junior program, Joe beat Arthur consistently," Whirlwind noted after Ashe's victory against Williams. "But Joe's poor mechanics finally caught up with him. Ashe has perfect mechanics. Arthur never demonstrated any temper or emotional signs of disgust. Often when he misses an easy shot, he smiles instead of slamming his racket. His calmness unnerves his opponents."

Though only a high school junior, Ashe already had proven himself to be a major talent by white standards as well. He was the No. 8 seed at the USLTA Interscholastic Championships in Charlottesville in 1960 and came close to ousting top-seed Billy Lenoir of Arizona in the quarterfinals. Unfortunately, Ashe lost the match mainly because of his inability to shake off a questionable decision he made that allowed Lenoir to climb back into the match. Whirlwind, who watched "good sport" Ashe crumble internally, described Ashe's decision in an ATA program.

Ashe won the first set and was leading 4-3 in the second set and on game point of the eighth game, Arthur won the game with a short ball that Lenoir couldn't reach. While trying for the ball, another ball came onto the court behind Lenoir that he didn't even see. While at the net, Arthur asked

KING ARTHUR

Lenoir if that ball had interfered with him. Lenoir looked back, saw the ball and said 'The referee said to always play a point over if a ball comes on the court from another court.' The score would have been 5-3 in favor of Ashe if he had kept his big mouth shut. They played the point over, Lenoir won the point, the game, the set and the next set because Ashe had lost his concentration, thinking about what it had cost him for opening his mouth, something he rarely does while playing. He did not win but two more games. He lost the biggest opportunity of his lifetime.

The heartbreaking loss, which clearly was more distressing to Whirlwind than it was to Ashe, didn't stop Ashe from enjoying a remarkable year. He beat several top-ranked USLTA juniors, including Herb Fitz Gibbon of Garden City, New York, and Hugh Lynch. Ashe's victory against Fitz Gibbon in the New Jersey State final was a testament to Whirlwind's near flawless ability to provide Ashe with the right strategy against most top players. Whirlwind knew that Fitz Gibbon, a lanky beanstalk, was physically stronger than Ashe, but Ashe had superior stamina. Here's Whirlwind's account of Ashe's upset victory against Fitz Gibbon:

Fitz Gibbon had defeated Ashe in the [USLTA National Championships] his first year at Kalamazoo. He is an uncanny net rusher and is over six feet tall. Arthur could not pass him at the net. He was telegraphing his shots. I told Arthur not to try to pass Fitz Gibbon in this match, but try to keep him away from the net with deep balls. When he did come to the net, I told Arthur to lob deep and try to return every smash. This he did.

He lost the first set to Fitz Gibbon 6-1, but kept lobbing. He lost the second set, 6-1. Spectators thought he was dumb. He had reached the final by passing shots and now he was losing by lobbing. He was behind 4-1 in the third set when Fitz Gibbon started to weaken and miss his overhead shots. That was the signal for Ashe to start passing him. Arthur won the third set 7-5, the fourth set 6-1 and the fifth set 6-0.

Ashe never strayed from Whirlwind's game plans. "I always did exactly what Dr. Johnson told me to do," Ashe said. "Usually, his strategy was right. Against Hugh Lynch in a tournament in Clifton Park in Baltimore, Doc told me to hit every ball to his backhand, which I did. The next time I played him he was expecting me to do the same thing, but Doc told me not to and the change worked. I beat him easily. Doc used to tell us that we shouldn't walk on the court unless we had a plan, something to do."

Relying on a strong first serve and flawless ground strokes, Ashe finished 1960 as one of the nation's rising junior stars. Whirlwind wouldn't let him develop a serve-and-volley game until he was 16. Ashe once said his delayed start at net training caused him to be an erratic serve-and-volleyer as a pro. His game was hampered more dramatically because of racial bias in the Southern sections. A prime example of the obstacles he faced occurred in 1960 when he defeated Jim Busick 4-6, 6-0, 6-1, 6-1 in the final for the Maryland State Junior title. The victory should have guaranteed Ashe a spot in the Middle Atlantic Championships, but he wasn't ranked in that region because USLTA officials refused to honor his request for entry in Middle Atlantic tournaments, despite his excellent record, which included his victory against Busick. Moreover, Ashe was never allowed to compete in USLTA events in his hometown of Richmond.

In August 1960, Ashe, then 17, defeated Wilbert Davis to win his first of two ATA National men's singles championships and openly talked of his desire to be the best in the world. But Whirlwind realized that too many Southern tennis officials adamantly refused to recognize Ashe's achievements, much less his potential. He knew, too, that they would try to derail, not help, Ashe's bid to reach the top of the tennis world. Whirlwind had no choice but to make his move.

17

Victory at Charlottesville

WHIRLWIND BROKE THE NEWS to his protégé in a phone conversation in late August 1960:
"I've made arrangements for you to live in St. Louis."

His words struck Ashe like a punishing body blow, leaving him wobbly and dazed. Away from tennis, Ashe, 17, had grown accustomed, if not comfortable, with life in his hometown. His neighborhood, family and school friends had provided a balance—indeed a haven—from the life he led as a gifted black who fate had picked to be a racial pioneer. Ashe's father shared his son's disappointment about him not being able to finish high school in Richmond. However, both realized—as Whirlwind did—that Richmond's racial policies most likely would prevent Ashe from realizing his full potential. And both knew that Whirlwind was thinking not just of Ashe's future, but also of the future of young Arthurs to be.

A high school junior, Ashe had come to realize that destiny demanded special sacrifices of those chosen to achieve special goals. He had been reminded of that a year earlier when his school principal kicked him off the baseball team, not because he lacked good baseball skills but because his priority should have been to develop his extraordinary talent in tennis.

Whirlwind knew, too, that danger lurked ahead for those seeking a quick change to the ways of the South. In February 1960—indeed a few months before the ATA National Interscholastic Championships were held on North Carolina A&T College's campus—four freshmen students at the predominantly black institution in Greensboro, N.C., sat down at a lunch counter in a local F.W. Woolworth store and waited to be served. When told to get up and move on, they opened their textbooks and gave the white South its most publicized lesson in a new form of civil disobedience.

Aided by an aggressive national media, news of the "sit-in" demonstration swept across the nation overnight. Within days, black college students at Fisk University in Nashville, Tennessee A&I, Hampton Institute and others used similar tactics at segregated lunch counters near their respective campuses. Even Whirlwind, then 60, joined black students in picket lines outside Lynchburg's F.W. Woolworth. "I remember once he was telling me how good he felt inside, being out there with the students demonstrating, walking the picket line," Bobby Jr. said. "He kept saying how good it made him feel."

Whirlwind felt even better, however, getting Ashe out of the South and providing him with the opportunity to be the very best that he could be. Richard Hudlin, a former captain of the Chicago University tennis team and one of Whirlwind's longtime allies, welcomed Ashe to his St. Louis home with open arms. The scenery was different—much colder, of course, in the winter—but Ashe's training routine remained the same. During his six previous summers in Lynchburg, Ashe had his every move regulated and controlled by Whirlwind, who pushed him often to the brink of what he could handle. Whirlwind was his coach, mentor and substitute father. Ashe never dared defy his father or Whirlwind, both of whom were stern taskmasters.

"Doc would make me hit 500 serves in the morning before I could have breakfast," Ashe said. "At times, I became so discouraged I wanted to quit, but Doc would always come up with an answer that kind of embarrassed me. One day he said, 'One quality of a champion is the ability to endure.'"

Like Whirlwind, Hudlin had a tennis court in his backyard, but Ashe spent nearly every day practicing against several other top-ranked juniors, including the Buchholz brothers, Butch and Cliff, on the wooden surface at the St. Louis Armory.

"Coming to St. Louis helped Arthur, no question," Butch Buchholz says, "the competition, environment and the fact that we all played tennis some days until we dropped."

The indoor facility made it possible for Ashe to do something he couldn't do in Lynchburg: play year-round. The quick surface also helped sharpen his reflexes and develop a strong serve-and-volley game, something he couldn't do in Lynchburg on Whirlwind's slow clay court. Ashe changed his grip, learned to put a little more punch in his serve and developed a topspin backhand. The changes lifted him to another level.

Ashe won his first national title, the junior indoors, in November 1960, upsetting Frank Froehling in a four-hour, five-set battle. Six months later and 10 years after embarking on an improbable mission, Whirlwind watched Ashe plant a flag of triumph on a once forbidden mountaintop. Standing head and shoulders above his challengers, top-seed Ashe waltzed through the field at the USLTA National Interscholastic Championships in Charlottesville without losing a set. He defeated Cliff Buchholz in the semifinals and Larry Parker in the final.

Whirlwind's decade-long frustrations, humiliations and disappointments—including Ashe's quarterfinal loss to Lenoir in 1960—were whisked away that week by the powerful serve and brilliant ground strokes of Ashe, his protégé who became the first black player to capture one of the nation's most prestigious junior events.

During the final weekend of that event, an invitation from several white friends—Cliff Buchholz, Charlie Pasarell and Butch Newman—reminded Ashe of why Whirlwind insisted that he leave the South.

"We were trying to go to this movie and they wouldn't let Arthur in," Cliff recalled. "Arthur said, 'What do you want me to do, paint myself with whitewash?' That was the only time I heard Arthur say anything about something he didn't like that was going on. At the time, he didn't want to make waves and didn't want to deal with a lot of pressure."

Ashe was pleased that his white friends refused to go inside the theatre after he was rejected. "I think we went to play pool instead," Buchholz said.

Whirlwind's dream-come-true ending apparently was a nightmare too horrible for Charlottesville tennis officials to live through again.

WHIRLWIND

The following year, the National Interscholastic Championship, which had been held in Charlottesville since 1946, was moved to Williamston, Massachusetts.

Ashe completed a most productive year in St. Louis by graduating as salutatorian of Sumner High School. He finished his senior year with a straight A average, but wasn't allowed to graduate as the valedictorian because he had been there for only a year. Michigan State, Hampton Institute and Arizona were among the colleges offering him full scholarships.

But the nation's premier junior player wanted only to attend UCLA, the nation's premier college for tennis players. Near the end of the summer, J.D. Morgan, UCLA's coach, made the call—and the pitch—that Ashe had waited patiently to receive. Actually, Ashe agreed to head West even before Morgan could complete a sentence.

A month before trotting off to the West Coast, Ashe captured his second consecutive ATA National singles title and then teamed with Ronald Charity to capture the ATA doubles crown. It was the first national title won by Charity, the man who gave Ashe his first tennis lesson on public courts less than 20 yards away from Ashe's Richmond home. Though they agreed to defend their title the next year, Ashe discovered that he had been teamed with Whirlwind, instead of Charity, in the 1962 ATA National doubles competition. Whirlwind wanted only to enjoy the same sentimental trip that Charity took last year while playing with Ashe. He knew that Ashe probably would never play another ATA event after this year. He saw this as a last opportunity to play with the boy who had become as special as a son. But Charity didn't see it that way.

"I found Arthur and I said, 'Hey man, what's going on?'" Charity said. "Arthur said, 'Mr. Charity—he never called me Ron—I don't know; you'll have to ask Dr. Johnson.'

"Well, I went to Bertram Baker and said, 'Look, I sent in an entry with Ashe and myself as partners; we're the defending champs.' Baker told me that Dr. Johnson told him to change it. I said, 'How can Dr. Johnson make you change my entry?'

"He went through this thing. He said, 'We apologize; we'll let you get another partner.' I said, 'I'll be damned.' That was the only thing I could do. I couldn't blame Ashe; he was only a 17-year-old kid caught in the middle. I thought that it was the worst thing in the world to happen. So I played with John Mudd, and as fate would have it, we played Johnson and Ashe in the first round and beat the hell out of them, 6-0, 6-1. I didn't hit a single ball to Arthur."

Whirlwind, who was 63, had slowed considerably and couldn't protect himself against hard-hitters like Charity and Mudd. Fans who watched the match admired Whirlwind's spirit, but pitied his performance. Charity and Mudd repeatedly bounced stinging forehand and backhand drives off his arms and chest. Mudd suggested they stop using Whirlwind as target practice, but Charity vetoed that idea unequivocally.

"I said to John Mudd, 'If you hit one ball to Arthur, I'll beat you to death with this racket right here on this tennis court.'"

Still miffed after the match, Charity confronted Whirlwind, demanding to know why he changed the pairings.

"Whirlwind said, 'Oh man, you had your chance to play with him; I just wanted to play with him,'" Charity said.

Though separated by more than 3,000 miles, Whirlwind continued to influence Ashe's career decisions in tennis—as a benefactor and a mentor—throughout his years at UCLA. Whirlwind raised funds to help Ashe make his first trip to Wimbledon in London, England, in 1963. Whirlwind begged and borrowed from his friends. Beth Lee, wife of one of Whirlwind's friends, solicited donations from white tennis fans watching matches at the Carter Baron Tennis Courts at 16th and Kennedy Streets in Washington, D.C. Lee collected more than $200.

In a proposal to the all-black Pigskin Club in Washington, D.C., Whirlwind stated that if the club donated half the sum needed to send Ashe to Wimbledon, he'd contribute the other half. Whirlwind, who had joined the sports-minded club in the 1940s, vehemently denounced the Club's decision to reject his proposal.

In a letter to the Club, Whirlwind said, "Each of 600 men who are known for their financial resources and love of athletics received letters of appeal and although over $100 was spent making the contacts by mail, not a single member of this famous club donated one cent to the program. Everybody wants to see a Negro on the Junior Davis Cup team, but few want to pay for it. Everybody commends Dr. Johnson on the fine work he's doing and the success of the team, but they all keep their money in their pockets."

Ashe never missed a rung in his climb to the top. While attending UCLA, he was selected to the Junior Davis Cup team in 1962 and the Davis Cup team in 1963. Whirlwind, who structured Ashe's game as a junior, still could pinpoint and correct flaws better than anyone else, even after he became a world-class player. Whirlwind knew, too, when to offer advice and when to keep his distance.

"After a major loss, he would phone long distance and analyze with me why I lost," Ashe said. "If I won, he wouldn't call, except to warn me against overconfidence. He also had a way of burning up the phone lines to advise me in key matches. In 1965, I played Roy Emerson, the No. 1 player in the world, in the U.S. National singles at Forest Hills. I won the first two sets, and then lost the third set, double faulting at set point.

"During the intermission, I remembered something Dr. Johnson had told me before the match. He said, 'Don't try for too many service aces. Tone down your first serve.' Following his advice, I came back relaxed and outlasted Roy to win the fourth set and the match—the biggest victory of my life up to that point."

Whirlwind monitored Ashe's tournament schedule and kept ATA members informed of his achievements through the organization's souvenir program, distributed each year at the National Championships. Ashe's picture often appeared on the cover of many ATA programs beginning in 1959. He was Whirlwind's ideal, the perfect junior for his era. Ashe's success made it easier for Whirlwind to recruit the next wave of black juniors, but it also stirred resentment and discontent among those who lost top talent to Whirlwind's program. Luis Glass of Jackson Heights, New York, and Linwood Simpson, of Wilmington, North Carolina, and Bonnie Logan of Durham, North Carolina, were among the black juniors on the rise, hoping to equal, if not surpass, the accomplishments of pioneers Ashe and Gibson.

18

You Go, Girls

WITH HIS GOAL OF GUIDING a junior male to the USLTA National Interscholastic singles title finally achieved, Whirlwind saw no reason why others could not follow in Ashe's footsteps. The Glass brothers, Luis and Sidney, and Linwood Simpson were among several promising young junior boys invited to join his camp. Sidney won the ATA National 12-and-under title in 1959, Luis claimed it in 1960 and Simpson snatched it in 1962. A few years later, Bonnie Logan, a 12-year-old girl from North Carolina, convinced Whirlwind that she, too, had world-class potential.

Whirlwind's emphasis in the '60s remained on developing boys, but several girls, including Logan, trained on Johnson's backyard court. Despite Althea Gibson's remarkable results, ATA officials, including Whirlwind, were slow to push girls into competitive tennis. A junior boy's event was included on ATA schedules in 1924; a separate event for girls was added in 1935. Whirlwind launched the ATA National Black Interscholastic Championships for boys in 1952. The ATA Interscholastic Championships for girls, which drew only eight players, was first held in 1954.

Beverly Coleman of Los Angeles, Ethel Reid Miller of Lynchburg and Gwen McEvans of Detroit were among the first group of girls invited to join Whirlwind's program. McEvans won the ATA National girls' title in 1957 and was considered the most promising player among the girls in the '50s.

"My father was always thinking ahead," Bobby Jr. said. "For example, the day Althea won the Wimbledon title in 1957, the first thing he said was, 'We got to get Gwen McEvans ready next.' That girl could play, but Gwen had her head somewhere else. She dropped out of the program."

Coleman, the first female invited to join Whirlwind's camp, spent the summer of 1955 in Lynchburg, but didn't return. Miller, who lived across the street from Whirlwind, began begging for lessons when she was 11. "I used to get up at 6. a.m. and walk over to his court and watch the boys play," Miller said. "I used to bug them about letting me play. I was persistent. One day, Dr. Johnson started teaching me the basics. I played in my first tournament the next year and I believe I won it."

Miller, the lone female in Whirlwind's camp in 1958-59, was almost immediately dubbed with a domestic title: Mother Ethel. She played the role.

"I did the lunch-making and cleaned up the kitchen after everyone had messed it up," she said. "When the Glass brothers came to Lynchburg, I had to take care of them. Not that I minded doing it, but I had to, among other things, break up their fights."

At the time, neither black girls nor white girls were encouraged to be athletes. As pre-teens, girls generally played with dolls. Once in high school, they were pushed gently to take home economics or join cheering squads. They went to college in search of husbands more often than degrees.

"The attitude in Lynchburg was that tennis was a boy's game," Miller said. "I won the Negro high school state singles and doubles championships in 1959 and nothing was said about it at school. I don't believe half the students knew about it. I didn't get any scholarship offers or anything. I didn't think Dr. Johnson had any confidence in girls, but then when I started winning tournaments, he said 'Hey, this might work.'"

Whirlwind rarely overlooked a player with talent—male or female—though it was more difficult for him to train and develop young girls. Providing separate housing for the girls was chief among his problems. In the '60s, his program averaged 10-12 players each summer. Girls invited during those first few years stayed across the street with Miller's family or with Whirlwind's friends or relatives. Female chaperones traveled with the team whenever young girls were in the group.

Whirlwind's experience with Ashe, combined with his exposure to junior development in white America, convinced him that juniors with the potential for greatness must give up large chunks of their childhoods in order to become tennis champions. Whirlwind searched for and recruited juniors with great potential, regardless of gender. In 1960, he believed he found a rising star in Durham, North Carolina. Ten-year-old Bonnie Logan bounced around those red clay courts displaying the arsenal of a seasoned pro. Logan's older brother, George, taught his sister to play. None of her girlfriends played; so Logan spent her early years battling the boys. "I was the only girl in Durham playing tennis," Logan said. "I used to have to go up to the college (North Carolina Central) and play against the boys. There weren't any girls playing who could really play."

Logan, like Althea Gibson, was a proud I-can-do-anything-a-boy-can-do tomboy. She loved to compete with boys in any sport. "I played all sports: basketball, football and baseball," she said. "(But) I decided I wanted to be a professional tennis player after I won my first trophy when I was 10. I felt tennis was a sport in which girls could excel."

Her exposure to tougher competition then, not later, would make Bonnie a national champion, Whirlwind decided. He remembered that Ashe's father was reluctant to let his 11-year-old son spend an entire summer away from home; so he wasn't surprised when Logan's parents initially dismissed his proposal. But Whirlwind didn't give up.

He included a picture of Logan holding two arms full of trophies in the 1961 ATA program. The caption, written by Whirlwind, read, "Bonnie needs coaching and play against USLTA players. If her parents would let her join the team, this 11-year-old girl has the potential of becoming a national champion in either league (ATA or USLTA) and it all depends on what league her parents keep her in."

Whirlwind's wily use of the power of the media worked. The following year, Logan became the first 12-year-old girl to join Whirlwind's program. During her first summer of training, Logan won eight major titles in various categories. Though only 12, she won the women's singles, girls' 18s and 15s at an event in Winston-Salem. She won a girls' 18s singles title in Baltimore, the Maryland State 14s and an 18s ATA title in Washington, D.C.

WHIRLWIND

She won the USLTA National girls' 12s in 1963, but lost that crown when she was declared ineligible after tournament officials discovered that she was born a few months before the cutoff date for that division. Her disappointment about that incident was washed away a month later when she was presented the *Sports Illustrated* Award of Merit, which was comparable to the USLTA National 12-and-under award. At 14, Logan was ranked No. 10 in the nation in the 16-and-under division. She captured her first ATA National women's singles title in 1964 and successfully defended that title six consecutive years, falling three years short of Gibson's record 10 consecutive ATA singles crowns.

Hoping to expose her to the nation's top junior girls talent, Whirlwind entered Logan in the 1964 U.S. National Girls' Junior Championships at Forest Hills, New York. He then discovered that others in the ATA were steering Logan in another direction.

"My father was sitting in the stands waiting for Bonnie to play in the USLTA Nationals," Bobby Jr. said. "He had paid her entry fee and saw her name in the draw. A lady came up to him and asked, 'Dr. Johnson, where is Bonnie? She's suppose to be playing now.' He said, 'I don't know.' Turns out that an ATA official in Durham, Carl Easterling, I believe, had decided that Bonnie should stay in Durham and play in the first integrated Raleigh-Durham tournament. They thought that was more important than Bonnie playing in the Nationals. My father said, 'You know, I can't help anybody if they don't show up.' "

In the early '60s, it seemed that criticism of Whirlwind's program was directly related to its success. Jealousy rode every victory lap made by Ashe, then a top collegiate star at UCLA, and by Logan, then a rising junior star. Hubert Eaton, elected ATA president in 1960—and one of Whirlwind's closest allies—couldn't stop the barrage of verbal attacks on his vice president, who had created and developed the organization's most publicized program. Instead of praise, Whirlwind mainly was pummeled each year at ATA meetings. Bobby Jr. noted the 1962 ATA gathering in Wilberforce was especially hostile:

The whole meeting was centered on the junior development program. People were disgruntled and annoyed that their hometown players weren't getting the shots, weren't being selected to the program. I remember Joe Williams even got up and complained. He resented the fact that Ashe and

Whirlwind, left, greets Hampton Institute captain before 1922 game.

Lincoln's 1923 Football Squad. Whirlwind is on first row, front and center with football.

Whirlwind, a basketball star for Omegas at Lincoln U.

Mama Nancy and Papa Jerry in Plymouth in the 1920s

Whirlwind and second wife, Hallie, lean on fender of Whirlwind's first car, a 1933 Buick. Mama Nancy is in the car and Papa Jerry is at far right.

From left, Jack Marsh, Louis Graves, former USLTA champion Bobby Riggs. Whirlwind and Chuck Jones, take break from game on Whirlwind's backyard court in Lynchburg, VA.

Victor Miller, left, and Roosevelt Megginson, first blacks to play in the USLTA Interscholastic Championships in Charlottesville, Va. (1951).

Whirlwind's mischievous duo

Horace Cunningham, 17

Billy Neilson, 17

Donald Dell, left, defeated ATA champion William Winn at 1953 USLTA scholastic tournament in Charlottesville, Va.

Willis Fennell, right, ATA junior champion from California junior, lost to Crawford Henry at 1955 Charlottesville event.

Whirlwind's home at 1022 Pierce Street in Lynchburg, Va. Clay court was in rear.
(Photo by Doug Smith)

Whirlwind, at right, and son, Bobby, Jr. They were the first blacks to play in the USLTA Father/Son events.

Seven-time ATA mixed doubles champions Whirlwind Johnson and Althea Gibson, on right, after defeating George Stewart and Ora Washington in 1948 final.

Whirlwind watches partner, Althea Gibson smash an overhead.

Members of Whirlwind's 1959 ATA Junior team.
From left, Charles Brown, Arthur Ashe, Ethel Reid, Hubert Eaton, Jr., and Joe Williams.

Don Budge, left, first player to win Grand Slam, greets ATA Champion Jimmie McDaniel after exhibition in Harlem.

Thousands gather at Harlem's Cosmopolitan Club in 1941 to watch Don Budge and Jimmie McDaniel in first interracial match.

one or two others got to play in USLTA tournaments and he never got that opportunity. My father sat there and took it all. He didn't make any attempt to vindicate himself vocally. I couldn't take it so I walked out.

My father did say later, 'Now, you heard Joe complaining. He doesn't realize that I kept him with my program long after his junior years were over. Joe was still with me when he was 21 and never realized that he wasn't eligible to be on a junior development program. I kept sponsoring him because he was a good guy and was a good practice partner for the other players.'

While Logan was Whirlwind's most gifted junior girl, she wasn't his best. Leslie Allen, who was only 10 when she made her first visit to Whirlwind's camp, became, in 1981, the first black woman since Gibson to win a tour event. She reached a career-best No. 17 on the WTA Tour before retiring in the early 1990s.

"As a kid with parents who played ATA events, I grew up in the ATA," Allen said. "When my mother sent me to Dr. J's, I knew I was going to a place of tradition, and when Dr. J spoke, we listened to him like he was the king. Even though we were very young, he instilled within us the importance of sportsmanship, calling your own lines, maintaining a good attitude and a sense of responsibility. It was a nurturing environment. You knew that everyone had your best interests at heart and you never felt threatened because someone was better than you. What I like most about his approach was he made it simple for you to understand what you had to do to get better, and a lot of it wasn't about stroke production.

"Althea Gibson came by one day and I was so in awe of her I couldn't look at her. I kept my head down. She had such a presence, like royalty. Sometimes Dr. J would tell us stories about Althea, Arthur, Bonnie and some of the older kids who were in the elite group and made the road trips. I wasn't in that group."

Whirlwind was in his 60s when Allen arrived, and because of continuous squabbles with ATA officials, one his closest friends, William "Babe" Jones of Baltimore, repeatedly urged him to walk away from the junior program. "Let them (ATA officials) have the program and run it like they want to," Jones told Whirlwind. "You can come out here, enjoy yourself and have a big time."

WHIRLWIND

Whirlwind held on to the program, but relinquished some responsibilities. In 1965, O.G. Walker of Lawrenceville, Virginia, became the team's traveling coach. Whirlwind, then 65, sensed that his impact as an ATA leader was beginning to fade. He wanted desperately for his achievements to be properly recognized, and he felt that would happen only if he moved up a notch and became the ATA's next president. So he implemented his secret plan.

19

New Attitude

ELECTED FIRST VICE PRESIDENT of the ATA in 1950, Whirlwind stood next in line to be the organization's president. But 16 years later, he was still first vice president. His feud with Bertram Baker and other ATA officials had made him unacceptable, in the eyes of others, for the position he yearned to hold.

"Whirlwind always wanted to be president of the ATA, but not for personal gain," his friend Dr. Hubert Eaton said. "He would twist arms, tell a little white lie, whatever was necessary always for his boys, always to promote his junior development program. People knew what he would do and everybody liked him, but they didn't want him to be head of the organization."

A former member of the ATA's executive committee called "pettiness" one of Whirlwind's most unattractive qualities.

"One time he voted me off the committee because I didn't vote with him," the former member said. "He said, 'Why didn't you vote with me?' And I would tell him that I vote for what I think is right. He never had the power he wanted. He was very power crazy. He had to have whatever he wanted."

In 1960, Whirlwind helped elect Eaton, his long-time ally, president. Six years later, Whirlwind asked Eaton to return the favor.

"I suspected it all the time," Eaton said. "Whirlwind came out and frankly admitted to me that he wanted to be president of the American Tennis Association. And I said, 'Well, Whirlwind, I didn't want it in the first place. The only reason I'm here is because you persuaded me to take it. So you know it's all right with me.' "

Whirlwind then told Eaton that he had arranged for another friend to nominate him for president during the election of officers at the ATA annual meeting.

"I said, 'Well, Whirlwind, you put me in a bad spot. I don't feel like I can just turn my back on all the people who have supported me over the years, but when it comes time for the election of officers, I think I'll just leave the room and that'll leave you to have freedom to operate.' I discussed this with my wife at the time. My position was that if the people there didn't want Whirlwind and there was nobody else, I just felt I shouldn't say, 'No, I'm not going to run.' "

Whirlwind had asked Dr. Herman 'Buck' Neilson, who was Hampton Institute's athletic director and Billy Neilson's father, to nominate him for president. The election of officers was the last item on the agenda.

"Mrs. Lucille Freeman, chairman of the nominating committee, opened the floor for nominations for president," Eaton said. "Buck was sitting up there, you know when he came to the tournament, and he was high most nights. So he was sitting up there looking over his glasses. So I called for the nominations of officers. I was nominated, and Mrs. Freeman wrote my name up there on the board. So I said, 'The chair will now entertain nominations from the floor.' Well, that was when Buck was supposed to stand up. I knew Buck was the one who was supposed to do it, but nobody else knew it because I was the only one Whirlwind told. I was expecting Buck to say something. So I said it twice. Then I said it again, 'Are there any other nominations for president?' Buck just sat there and didn't open his damn mouth. Whirlwind was sitting in the back; so I couldn't say anything. Nothing I could do at that point. I don't recall how we did it, but that put me back in office."

Whirlwind's quiet coup attempt fizzled mainly because Neilson forgot his lines.

"Whirlwind gave Buck hell," Eaton said. "He said, 'Dammit, you promised me last night that you were going to nominate me for president.' Buck said, 'I did? I don't remember that, man.' "

NEW ATTITUDE

By the mid-'60s, Whirlwind discovered that ATA officials weren't the only ones determined to deny him the control he craved. Many black youngsters, including some attending Whirlwind's camp, found comfort and kinship in the black leaders who offered a more strident response to racism, instead of the turn-the-other-cheek philosophy advocated by Whirlwind and other black leaders who preached nonviolence.

Though the Rev. Martin Luther King Jr. eventually won the Nobel Peace Prize for his forgive-thy-white-neighbor method of combating racial discrimination, Malcolm X, who preached the gospel according to Elijah Muhammad of the Nation of Islam, won the hearts and minds of inner-city youths with a far more strident, send-them-to-the-cemetery message. The gun-toting Black Panther Party, formed in October 1966, sprang from the grave of Malcolm X. Neither Malcolm X, who was assassinated in February 1965, nor Huey Newton, who co-founded the Black Panther Party with Bobby Seale, ever encouraged blacks to curry favors from the white power structure. Newton talked "of political power growing out of the barrel of a gun."

Given a choice of divergent black voices—King or Malcolm X—mainstream America chose King, who was assassinated in April 1968. President Lyndon B. Johnson signed and pushed through Congress important civil rights legislation in 1964 that helped blacks participate more fully in the American mainstream. More significantly, the struggle prompted blacks to re-examine their value systems as they became more comfortable with the face they saw in the mirror each morning.

Black men and women no longer were ashamed of their kinky hair, big noses and full lips. Many stopped using chemicals or hot combs to straighten their hair. The Afro hairstyle became a badge of pride. They wore dashikis and emphasized their unanimity with clinched fist salutes. They no longer wanted to be called Negroes, which is Spanish for black. Singer James Brown's *"I'm black and I'm proud"* became the black community's rallying cry.

Whirlwind found himself with more defiant juniors at his camp than he had known in the '50s. They were extremely talented and eager to be world-class tennis players, but they rejected Whirlwind's requests that they be subservient or docile in the presence of whites. "I didn't like putting up with that Uncle Tom stuff," said Horace Reid, who won the ATA National men's title when he was 17 and spent a few weeks at Whirlwind's house in the late '60s.

Arthur Carrington, another top-ranked junior in the '60s, also spent a few confrontational weeks in Whirlwind's camp. The extensive training, travel, competition and other advantages associated with Whirlwind's junior program were useful, Carrington said. "But I couldn't relate to the etiquette lessons. I'm from Elizabeth, New Jersey, and I was brought up in a militant atmosphere," Carrington said. "I grew up listening to Malcolm X and other militant black speakers. I experienced an identity crisis when I was on the tour. I couldn't relate to white people. Dr. Johnson would send me to the black tournaments and the other guys to the white tournaments. He used to tell me that he didn't send me to any white tournaments because he thought I'd blow it, that socially, I had a bad attitude.

"I tried to tell him that he was going to be dealing with a new type of black player, with a new attitude and temperament. That's what happened to all the black players who came up during that time. Their progress was based on how much they would assimilate into the white structure. I used to tell Dr. Johnson that, 'Hey, I'm going to be the man.'"

People frequently referred to Carrington, the 1973 ATA men's singles champion, as "the next Arthur Ashe." Carrington never liked to be compared to Ashe, primarily because he associated the label with personality and felt strongly that he was dramatically different from Arthur as a personality. Carrington noted that Ashe's exposure to racism occurred during Ashe's childhood years, a fact he believes robbed Ashe of a true understanding of the psychological impact of being black in America. "Things that happened to him as a kid happened to me as a man," Carrington said. "And that's a different perspective."

While Carrington and Reid were young juniors on the rise, Ashe was hovering near the top. Still at UCLA, Ashe won the U.S. Hard Court Championship in 1963 and the U.S. Intercollegiate title in 1965. He was an Army officer stationed at West Point when he won the U.S. Clay Court Championship in 1967. The following year, Ashe put it all together to become the country's No. 1 player. He won 10 of 22 tourna-

NEW ATTITUDE

ments and 11 of 12 Davis Cup matches. In September 1968, Ashe became the first black man to capture the U.S. National singles title, and he also won the inaugural U.S. Open singles championship. (The two events merged in 1970.)

Not surprisingly, Whirlwind was in the stands at Forest Hills in 1968, relishing Ashe's stunning victory against Tom Okker of the Netherlands 14-12, 5-7, 6-3, 3-6, 6-3 in the U.S. Open final. Ashe's father joined him on court for the trophy presentation. Ashe Sr. shared the historic moment with tears in his eyes and his son's arm draped around his shoulders. That picture of the Ashes was carried in newspapers and magazines across the country.

Whirlwind joined the Ashes at courtside, but stayed in the background while they posed for the cameras. The moment, Whirlwind knew, belonged to father and son, yet he felt a father's joy and pride as he watched the younger Ashe beam brightly as he stood atop the tennis world. Whirlwind beamed, too, and shared vicariously in the success of the young man he had groomed daily for so many years, believing all the while that this moment would come. He realized, too, that he had loved Arthur Ashe as much as he had loved his own children. Whirlwind spent some quality moments with his children—Carolyn Waltee and Bobby Jr. But the attention that he devoted to them paled in comparison to the time he spent with his program—and especially with Ashe. Waltee and Bobby Jr. competed for their father's love and affection, but deep inside, realized all the while that theirs would always be, to some degree, a losing battle.

20

Father-Daughter

WHEN SHE WAS A LITTLE GIRL, Carolyn Waltee Johnson Moore looked upon Whirlwind as an ideal daddy, a respected professional and a man of varied interests and talent.

"He had so many hobbies and he was so diverse," Waltee said. "I could say that my father plays tennis; I could say that my father goes fishing; I could say that my father goes hunting; I could say that my father likes to take pictures and develop them. There were just so many things he could do."

Despite the frequent weekend travel demanded by his junior program, along with his workload, Whirlwind often found time for his daughter. Sometimes, she became a companion in his busy life. "I'd go hunting with him," she said. "I'd jump on the bushes and make the birds come up and he'd shoot them. I'd help in the darkroom, develop films. He'd do all the big things with the equipment or whatever he'd use, but he'd have me stir the trays. I'd be the ball boy when we'd go to tournaments. I had my little white shorts, socks and shoes. I was very young, but I liked being with my dad. I admired him quite a bit."

Tucked away in her mind's eye, Waltee stored a treasure chest of special memories—large and small—with her daddy. She shared with him the kinds of things that have turned fathers everywhere into mush in the hands of their little darling daughters.

I'd lay his pajamas out at night and pull back the covers on his bed. Sometimes, I would stand in the bathroom door watching him shave while we talked about things. He would tell stories about the time he was a red-

cap at Grand Central Station and the hard times he had when he was going to school. He'd talk about the sacrifices he made, like putting his slacks under the mattress to press them because he didn't have an iron.

When I was five years old, my grandmother, Mother Nancy, and I would go with him on house calls. We would sit in the car and wait for him. Sometimes, we'd go way out in the countryside. Seemed like a long way to me. Sometimes, I'd carry his bag. He'd always stop and talk to people. He'd smile and have a nice conversation with them. He was very sensitive and always seemed interested in what people had to say.

I remember going to the grocery store with him. I was just learning to cook and liked to use spices. I would ask him to buy things we already had and he'd get them just to please me. I felt closest to him during those years when I was pulling the cover back on his bed and laying out his pajamas. That's when I was 12 to 14. I was always trying to do things that would endear me to him. He told me that he really did appreciate me trying to do that, and that's all I needed to hear. I don't think people really knew how much I loved my father. To me, he was mother and father.

Born in 1941, Waltee came into Whirlwind's life just as his marriage to Peggy was deteriorating. Peggy moved back home to Thomaston, Georgia, after she and Whirlwind separated in 1945.

"I don't recall my mother ever living in Lynchburg with us," Waltee said. "If she did, I was very young. Mainly, I remember people taking care of me or me going to live in different places. That's why I always tried to get his love and attention. I felt like, at times, I wasn't wanted. I mean, I felt I was wanted, but I didn't have the closeness of a mother and father relationship. When I went to visit my mother, I always was anxious to get back to see my daddy. When I was with daddy, I wanted to see how my mother was."

One thing Waltee could do without seeing, however, was Whirlwind deeply engrossed in his junior development program. Whirlwind's work ethic permeated the program. He spent as much time, maybe more, teaching his players about discipline and hard work as he did showing them how to hit great forehands and backhands. Waltee often grew testy when she saw her daddy spending so much time with the boys in his camp. "Waltee always used to talk about how those damn boys were taking her daddy away from her," Ethel Miller recalled.

Waltee didn't really care much for tennis and definitely didn't want to take lessons from her father as part of a group. "As long as I can remember there always was someone coming or going playing tennis at the house," Waltee said. "I was just not a person who was really interested in tennis. I was never really good. He was so involved in tennis. Being the type of personality I am, I just took a back seat and watched. I always wanted his wholehearted attention; so I didn't want to play. When he finished with everybody else, he would try to help me, and that's when we had our best times. I was eight years old."

Whirlwind never tried to coerce Waltee to play tennis, as he did Bobby Jr. "I think he felt, as far as tennis was concerned, most girls—after they got a certain age—just didn't have the interest," she said. "Not that he didn't think they had the ability; Althea showed that girls had the ability."

Althea began spending her summers at Whirlwind's home shortly before Waltee's seventh birthday. "I remember Althea playing the piano and singing at some of the parties," she said. "I would be upstairs in bed, but I could hear lots of people. They used to have some good times."

In her teen years, Waltee's attitude toward boys became less hostile. She learned to enjoy their company. Indeed, the time came when she preferred the attention of a boy to her father. "Whenever daddy took me to a tournament, I would spend all my time getting ready for the dances at night," Waltee said. "One year while preparing for a banquet in Wilberforce, I had my hair in rollers all day. That night, I went to the dance with daddy and Babe Jones. Daddy asked me to dance and—I don't know why—but I said no. Not long after that, a younger man—not a man, a fellow—asked me to dance and I said okay. My daddy saw that. I couldn't have been more than 15 years old.

"My daddy didn't ask me to dance with him again the rest of the night. I was hurt; I couldn't understand. I never realized what had happened."

Later, Whirlwind revealed his pain through a father-daughter chat that Waltee never forgot. "He told me that if someone asks you to dance," Waltee said, "don't refuse that person and then dance with someone else right away. That offended him, though I wasn't aware of it. It did teach me a lesson about how to be tactful. He always thought of the other person's feelings."

Whirlwind rarely found it necessary to punish his daughter, but she did recall receiving a few spankings as a child. "I got my last spanking when I was 11," she said. "At that age, I thought I knew everything. My sister-in-law, Nerissa, Bobby's wife, told daddy I was talking back to her and that she couldn't do anything with me. I think he considered it a favor that she was watching me, and he didn't want to have any problems. So he spanked me. I guess I had gotten a little grown. Most of the time, all he had to do was look at me. He had the kind of eyes that made you feel uneasy. He really didn't have much of a problem with me as far as behavior was concerned. I really wanted to please him."

Whirlwind tried desperately to please his children, too. Giving them frequent glimpses of life outside of Lynchburg earned him brownie points with Waltee.

We went to the World's Fair in New York, we went to movie theatres in New York, we saw the Harlem Globetrotters and we went to restaurants. I remember he wanted to take me to the Grand Ole Opry when it came to Lynchburg. He kept saying it would be almost like a historical thing for me to see, but I didn't want to go and I'm not sure if he went.

He did go to the March on Washington the year (1963) Martin Luther King gave his "I Have a Dream" speech. Daddy was very proud of that. It always makes me want to cry just thinking about how proud he was of being a part of that march. Daddy lived a sophisticated life and really enjoyed the cultured things in life. I think that's why he sent me to all those schools.

Whirlwind worked hard to upgrade the quality of education in the local black school system, but for Waltee and Bobby Jr., he followed the example of wealthy whites, opting to send his children to private schools. Both spent most of their secondary education years away from home. Bobby Jr. graduated from Palmer Memorial High School in Sedalia, North Carolina. Waltee attended Palmer in grades 5-8 and then left the country to complete grades 9 and 10 at St. Mary's Academy in Windsor, Canada. "Two years was enough, so we tried something different," said Waltee, who completed her high school education at Mather Academy in Camden, South Carolina. Later, she received an undergraduate degree, with a major in social studies, from Elizabeth City (North Carolina) College.

"Sometimes, I felt he was overly concerned about my schooling," she said. "Daddy wanted me to do well in school. He was disappointed when I didn't. He had a strong feeling that the salvation of black people would be obtained through education. He wanted us to go as far as we could. I don't think I lived up to expectations."

Whirlwind heightened Waltee's insecurities regarding education by comparing her grades and study habits to Ashe's. During those years, he frequently told her how well Ashe was doing in high school and in college at UCLA.

"At times, I could have almost hated Ashe," she said. "Maybe I didn't achieve as much as daddy thought I should have, but a lot of times, I would loved to have seen him come to show some interest in me. When I was graduating from college, where was daddy? Somewhere watching Ashe play tennis. When I came home to have my first baby in Lynchburg, so I could be close to daddy, where was he? In Florida, watching Ashe play tennis. I think daddy would have loved to have had Ashe for a son, not for fame, but because of his achievements."

Still, she admired and respected Ashe and once scolded her father for criticizing Ashe about losing focus during a tournament in Washington, D.C. "Daddy, Miss Creasy, Ashe and I were traveling together and daddy was fussing at Ashe about something," Waltee said. "I think he was trying to get a point across to Ashe about something he did in the match that was contrary to what daddy wanted Ashe to do. Ashe was driving. I can remember defending Ashe, telling daddy that maybe he shouldn't fuss at him so much. I don't remember what he said. Most likely he told me to be quiet."

Waltee envied Ashe mainly for providing her father with so many satisfying moments, in particular the 1968 U.S. Open. "Daddy was extremely proud of Arthur that day," she said. "But I think it was a tough moment for him when they called Ashe's father down to the court. Daddy stayed in the background, but I think he wanted to be out there next to Arthur."

Whirlwind saw very little of Ashe after 1968, and it seemed as if that victory had snapped the ties that had bound them together for so many years. But for a while, Whirlwind had difficulty letting Ashe loose.

"Ashe moved into another world," Waltee said. "I'm pleased that daddy had someone he was very proud of, regardless of how he felt about Ashe in the end. He was not bitter toward Ashe, but I think he felt Ashe had found people who Ashe thought had more to offer, more knowledge. I don't think he felt bad about Ashe. Maybe it was like a son who listens to the father, and then the son outgrows the father. And the father might stand back and say, 'Is it that he doesn't need me anymore? Is it that he doesn't still fit in my world?' I'm sure he had those kinds of feelings.

"I don't think Ashe realized the degree to which my father loved him. I thought he cared for Ashe more than he did for me. I thought he was prouder of Ashe than he was of me. I didn't have any of the accomplishments that Ashe had and I didn't want any competition like that. Bobby was a bit older than me, maybe he didn't have that same feeling."

21

Father-Son

BEFORE LITTLE BOBBY JR. could understand or appreciate feelings associated with having a father around the house, Whirlwind was gone. Born into a dying marriage, Bobby Jr. never felt the warmth of a mother and father working in unison to shower their child with unconditional affection.

Bobby Jr. was just a toddler when Whirlwind left home to attend medical school at Meharry. Annie and Whirlwind had lived separately for four years before their divorce, which was granted when Bobby Jr. was six years old. Annie remarried shortly after the divorce and was on a honeymoon trip when Whirlwind stormed into Goldsboro, North Carolina, grabbed Bobby Jr. away from his grandmother and took him to Lynchburg to live with him and his new wife, Peggy.

"I was sickly when I was a little boy," Bobby Jr. said. "It was decided that I should stay with my father. In those days, children didn't have anything to say about what was going on anyway."

In those days, Whirlwind wanted mainly for Bobby Jr. to follow in his footsteps, especially as an athlete. He took Bobby Jr. on hunting and fishing trips and played catch with him nearly every day. "My old man wanted me to be able to throw with either hand equally as well."

Bobby Jr. was nine when his father gave him his first tennis lesson. Whirlwind was only a few years out of medical school at the time and was still learning. "He was more interested in his own development as a player than he was in trying to develop me," Bobby Jr. said. "He was from the old school. He was very, very strict. He expected too much of everyone close to him."

At 14, Bobby Jr. learned the hardships associated with living with a father whose reputation as a ladies' man contributed to his stepmother's decision to look for happiness in another drink. At times, Bobby Jr. wasn't sure which he hated more: his stepmother's drinking or being forced by his father to call her "Mother Dear." Whirlwind and Peggy argued nearly every night, and for Bobby Jr., life at home at the time became an interminable nightmare.

"Lynchburg wasn't very nice to me," Bobby Jr. said. "It wasn't very pleasant being the son of a small town doctor who was married to an alcoholic. They were having problems and I was embarrassed. So I tried to stay away as long as I could."

Bobby Jr. attended Lynchburg's Dunbar High School during his freshman year, but spent the rest of his high school years at Palmer Memorial in Sedalia, North Carolina. Though his interest in tennis had grown considerably, Bobby Jr. even stayed away from Lynchburg during the summers. "I discovered the world of work," he said. "Instead of going home to play tennis, I waited on tables in Quantico (Virginia)."

Whirlwind and Peggy closed the book on their troubled marriage as Bobby Jr. headed to college: Prairie View State in Texas. Bobby Jr. looked forward to spending his summers at home, sharing life and the tennis court with his father. They played doubles together at ATA events during Bobby Jr.'s collegiate years, and in August 1950, they became the first blacks to participate in the USLTA National Father/Son Clay Court Tournament at the Erie Tennis Club in Erie, Pennsylvania. Whirlwind and son played in several other USLTA-sanctioned father/son events and in numerous ATA doubles tournaments as well. Their performances were occasionally solid, but rarely completed without heated volleys—of a verbal nature—between father and son.

Dr. Thomas Calhoun, a Washington, D.C.-based physician, recalled one such squabble. "Wilbur Jenkins and I played doubles against Dr. Johnson and Bobby in a tournament in Orlando, Florida, before the ATA Nationals one year," Calhoun said. "Unfortunately, the thing I remember most about it was the bickering on the court. I found it unsettling to see a father and son arguing on the court. Although we won the match, it was still unsettling. I came from a background where you just didn't talk back to your parents."

For the most part, a love of tennis, the one thing father and son had in common, brought out strands of discontent in one another. The tennis court for this father and son tandem seemed more like an emotional battlefield than a place where love and reason prevailed.

"The thing I really resented was that he'd always be telling me what to do," Bobby Jr. said. " 'You've got to get the first serve in. You've got to get to the service line for the first volley.' We'd be at the net together and the opponents would lob over him and at the last minute, when he realized he couldn't hit the overhead, he'd yell to me, 'Take it!' And I would have to run way back behind him and take it. I tell you it was something. I hated playing doubles with him. I hated it! But, you know, I'm a good doubles player in spite of my father. He taught me and he taught me well, but the agony of learning was just too much."

Bobby Jr.'s most agonizing moments occurred in their morning singles practices. Determined to win, Whirlwind employed guerilla warfare tactics against his son during those sessions.

What was really sadistic about it was before he'd go to the office in the morning, we'd play singles. He would do all sorts of things to distract me, to make me serve double faults. I mean, like he'd go to the net and towel off between my first and second serves. Sometimes, he would untie and then tie the strings on his shoes between my first and second serves. And then, when he'd come home in the evenings and we'd practice for the father/son tournaments, he'd be so upset because I was serving double faults. He'd say, 'My God, a double fault!' Those were some times.

But there were good times mixed in, times when even Whirlwind realized that their bond as father and son was far more important than any final score.

We had a lot of fellowship, a lot of fun. Each year about two weeks before returning to Prairie View, we'd have a championship match to determine who was the world champion, who was the best. He'd be in his world and I'd be in my mine. He taught me, and for years and years he beat me. But when I got to my late teens, I started getting the edge; I started beating him.

FATHER-SON

Bobby Jr., however, was never considered a rising star. Twice (1958 and 1961), he was selected by the ATA to play in the U.S. Nationals at Forest Hills. The ATA was supposed to recommend its singles champion and other top players to fill the four to six spots reserved for its players. Whirlwind, an ATA vice president, obviously pulled strings to have his son enjoy a day with the game's elite. More than 20 ATA players were ranked above Bobby Jr. when he enjoyed his second trip to Forest Hills in 1961. Being the son of a small town doctor with strong connections in the tennis world wasn't that bad.

"I recognized that I probably had a better opportunity than any other black person in the country to be a champion," Bobby Jr. said. "Didn't have the talent, wasn't thinking about it, but I was willing to work hard because I had a father who would support my chances to play."

Bobby Jr. left Prairie View State College in 1950 with a degree in physical education. He spent the next two years in the U.S. Army and then returned to Lynchburg with his wife, Nerissa. Whirlwind was as surprised and disappointed as Papa Jerry was when Whirlwind brought Annie to Plymouth as his wife.

"Dr. J used to call Bobby 'Chief' during that time," Nerissa said. "Bobby told me that shortly after we arrived in Lynchburg, Dr. J said, 'Chief, I thought you said we were going to be bachelors together, and here you are getting married.'"

Bobby Jr. and Nerissa moved into a five-room apartment inside the two-story office complex that Whirlwind had built at the corner of Fifth and Polk Streets. The building included Whirlwind's 10-room office suite, four apartments, a canteen for teenagers and several other businesses. Nerissa and Whirlwind's medical secretary and companion, Erdice Creasy, helped manage the canteen in the early '50s. Whirlwind had a two-way mirror installed in his private office, which allowed him to see inside the canteen, but people inside the canteen couldn't see him. "He had to be in control all the time," Nerissa said.

While his wife went to work each day, Bobby Jr. stayed at home to coordinate Whirlwind's junior development program. The arrangement worked perfectly for Whirlwind. Bobby Jr. responded to his father's requests as if they were direct orders. Nerissa, who was mostly ignored, was quite displeased with her father-in-law's control over her husband.

"Dr. J would tell him to do things, like, 'Take these kids to New York,' or 'Go pick up this car in Washington,' or 'Do this or that,'" Nerissa said. "I told Bobby, 'You can't just do whatever he says without talking to me. I'm your wife. You have to let me know what's going on.' I never liked being dependent upon Bobby's family because being dependent meant you had to dance to the music they played."

Whirlwind became more involved in the junior development program once Ashe established himself as the junior that Whirlwind had dreamed of finding. Besides, it gave Whirlwind the opportunity to help Bobby Jr. fulfill his father's other dream: to have his son become a doctor. Bobby Jr. was admitted to the Howard University School of Medicine in 1958. After successfully completing his first year, he moved Nerissa and family into a townhouse in Washington, D.C., that Whirlwind had purchased from his friend Stud Greene.

"I held the second mortgage on this house at 1725 S St. in Northwest," Greene said. "And I had just taken over the house because the man had gotten behind in his payments. I told Whirlwind that the man owed me $5,000-plus on the house and about $8,000 to Perpetual, who held the first mortgage. I said 'I'll let you have the house for the amount the man didn't pay me, about $5,000.' So he gave me that and took over the payments on the first mortgage."

Bobby Jr.'s dream of completing Howard's medical school ended soon after he and his family moved into their new home. He flunked out after the first semester of his second year. "There was too much conflict," said Bobby Jr., who accepted a teaching position in the D.C. school district soon afterwards.

Two years later, Bobby Jr. got a second chance at a medical degree when his aunt Dr. Eileen Eldorado (Dr. El) Johnson agreed to send him to her alma mater: the University of Geneva Medical School in Geneva, Switzerland. Whirlwind, who doted over his younger sister as if she were his child, had paid Dr. El's medical school expenses. Nerissa felt less threatened by Dr. El as Bobby Jr.'s sponsor and felt good about the arrangement. However, Dr. El soon found herself burdened by the expense of taking care of Bobby's Jr.'s educational and living costs, his D.C. mortgage payments and Nerissa's household needs. Whirlwind took over.

For the next three years, Nerissa raised their three children—Bobby III, Julian and Lance—while Bobby Jr. sought a medical degree in Switzerland. Whirlwind added stress to her life during the third year of Bobby Jr.'s absence by insisting on keeping Bobby III with him in Lynchburg. Whirlwind showered Bobby III with gifts and affection. "Every year, little Bobby would come home with a suitcase full of clothes," Nerissa said. "Dr. J gave him a rocking chair and a corncob pipe for Christmas. The other children felt left out."

After Christmas 1966, Nerissa decided that Bobby III would not return to Lynchburg with Whirlwind. She had tucked Bobby III in bed when Whirlwind came to get him.

"He came by on a Sunday to pick up little Bobby," Nerissa said. "When I told him little Bobby wasn't going back with him, he started ranting and raving like a madman. He took him anyway. The next day, I called a lawyer. I also called Bobby and threatened divorce."

When he returned home from Switzerland the next summer, Bobby Jr. walked into a wife who felt scorned by his father. Nerissa emphasized that little Bobby would not be going back to Lynchburg when Bobby Jr. returned to school in the fall. The arrangement, she said, was too divisive. Any other option, she said, would be determined in a divorce court. Whirlwind had no qualms about playing the money card in the dispute.

"Little Bobby told us that Aunt Eldorado and Aunt Elaine had said if Bobby didn't let him stay in Lynchburg, then Dr. J was not going to give him any more money," Nerissa said.

Whirlwind called Bobby Jr. from New York in early September to discuss his financial needs for the upcoming school year. "But before they talked about that, Dr. J asked Bobby, 'Are you going to let me keep little Bobby?' " Nerissa said. "Bobby said, 'No.' and then Dr. J said, 'Well, I'm through with you.' And that was it. We were cut off without a cent. Bobby Jr. didn't return to medical school."

Nerissa often wondered why Whirlwind would attempt to wreck his son's marriage over the matter. Years later, he offered an explanation.

"Little Bobby was just four years old at the time," Nerissa said. "Dr. J told me that that was the age Bobby was absent from his life and he was trying to relive through my son what he had missed with his own son."

Several of Bobby Jr.'s relatives were convinced that he left medical school because he had neither the ability nor the desire to be doctor. "You don't stay in medical school for four years and not want to be a doctor," he countered. "My father gave me a hard time. He didn't want me to grow up. He wanted to always be in charge."

Dr. Eaton, whose son, Hubert Jr., followed in his footsteps to become a physician, had unique insight into Whirlwind's relationship with Bobby Jr.

A boy who has to live in the shadow of a daddy who is well-known—no matter whether he's well-known in tennis, medicine or civil rights work—seems not able to accept the fact that he should be proud of his daddy and not feel that people think he should be doing the same thing that his daddy does.

Bobby wanted to be a doctor because his daddy was a doctor. Bobby knew doctors made a lot of money. Then Bobby was never Bobby Johnson, but always Whirlwind's boy. I see this pretty much in my own son. I'm pretty well-known up and down the East Coast. I think my son has developed some kind of attitude about people saying, 'Oh, you're Dr. Eaton's son.' Whirlwind always wanted the best for Bobby, whether he deserved it or not.

Nerissa said, "When Bobby Jr. didn't go back to medical school in Switzerland, every time we'd visit friends of Dr. J's they'd always say to me, 'So you're the one who didn't want your husband to go to medical school.'"

Whirlwind's friend's say he was deeply hurt when Bobby Jr. resumed his teaching career in the D.C. school district. Lucille Freeman, an ATA official whose sons, Clyde and Harold, also became physicians, said the decision destroyed Whirlwind's vision of his life upon retirement.

"Whirlwind had two dreams that were never realized," Mrs. Freeman said. "His unspoken dream was to be the president of the American Tennis Association. The one he often talked about was for Bobby Jr. to be a doctor and take over his practice in Lynchburg when he retired."

22

Dr. El

WITHOUT HIS FATHER'S FINANCIAL ASSISTANCE Bobby Jr. understood that a medical degree with his name on it would never hang from any of his walls. And Whirlwind realized that his dream of having his office stationery one day read 'Johnson & Son' would never be. He was content, however, to have it read 'Johnson & Johnson.'

Dr. Eileen Eldorado Johnson was employed at a New York hospital in 1967 when her oldest brother beckoned her to Lynchburg. Whirlwind told her that his practice had grown steadily and he had grown too old—he was 68—to manage it alone. Dr. El loved living in New York. She frequently attended concerts and the theater and felt at home strolling Fifth Avenue's broad sidewalks, mingling with the masses. She knew Lynchburg's Main Street would not only be several hundred miles away, but several lifestyles away as well. Still, she knew she had to go. She loved her big brother too much and felt that she owed him too much not to answer his cry for help.

From the very beginning, Mama Nancy and Papa Jerry encouraged the Johnson clan to help one another receive a quality education. Victoria, the clan's older sister, attended Elizabeth City Normal College, but a severe hearing problem hindered her desire to be a nurse. Sister Eva received a bachelor's of science degree from Hampton Institute and a master's degree from New York University. She was the principal of Short Journey Elementary School in Smithfield, North Carolina, for 44 years. "Don't laugh, but the school was named 'Short Journey' because it was a short journey from the Smithfield city limits," said Eva, chuckling.

Eva and Whirlwind sponsored younger brothers Roy, who attended Lincoln for two years, and Rupert, who finished North Carolina Central in Durham, North Carolina. Whirlwind provided both brothers with spending change and bought them clothes; Eva paid tuition and all other expenses. Whirlwind, alone, sponsored Dr. El, his youngest sister, who looked upon him more as a father than a brother.

Whirlwind was at Lincoln in 1922 when he learned that Mama Nancy had given birth to a baby girl. He had just finished studying the works of Edgar Allen Poe, which included the poem, *"In Search of Eldorado."* Whirlwind loved that poem and thought the name Eldorado would be perfect for his baby sister. Mama Nancy agreed.

By the time Eileen Eldorado turned 10, Whirlwind was an established physician in Lynchburg. She noticed that the older family members catered to her big brother. They talked of his achievements as a football player and as a doctor with gushing pride and admiration. They also sought his advice and relied on him to resolve many of the family's major problems. "If he said, 'that's right,' then that was right," Dr. El said. "All through my school years, I'd send him the papers I wrote, if I got A's on them. Luckily, I managed to get a few A's. He was old enough to be my father and I respected him as a father. We never had an argument. We had discussions, but we never got angry at each other. Never."

After receiving a bachelor's degree from North Carolina Central College, Eileen Eldorado seriously considered becoming a lawyer. Whirlwind giggled at the notion.

"If you want to starve, go to law school," he told her. "But if you go to medical school, I'll pay all your bills."

Said Dr. El, "He had such persuasive powers. He rarely raised his voice and yelled, but he could be emphatic. You knew when he meant something. As my mother used to say, 'You knew when he was not playing.'"

Eileen Eldorado began her quest for a medical degree at Howard University, but left in frustration after her first year. Even among blacks, the prevailing attitude in America in the late 1940s was that a woman's place was in the kitchen or the bedroom, not the classroom. Neither black men nor white men were prepared psychologically to deal with an assertive black woman striving to be an exception to the male-dominated world's rule of order. After learning that Europeans were more receptive to the idea of women becoming professionals, Eileen Eldorado attended the University of Geneva Medical School in Geneva, Switzerland.

"Eldorado and I were in school abroad during the same time," said Dr. Helen Edmonds of Durham. "She was my very good friend. I was at the University of Heidelberg in West Germany, and she was up in Geneva. She was there for about six years. I was about four hours away from her by train."

Edmonds and Eileen Eldorado often spent weekends together and occasionally visited other European countries, including Great Britain and France.

"I used to tease her by telling her I'd be there when Whirlwind's check came," Edmonds said. "She'd say, 'It doesn't matter because I know you're over here on a grant from the Ford Foundation; so we can make it.' But don't get the idea that she ever needed any money from me. Whirlwind kept her amply supplied. She had a four-room apartment in an excellent part of Geneva. She had maid service, a doorman, everything. It was hard to get into her building. I used to tell her that I hated to go out to the market when she wasn't there because it was always hard as the devil to get back in there."

Dr. El graduated from the Geneva Medical School in the late '50s and then took obstetrical training at the Rotunda Hospital in Dublin, Ireland. Later, she completed a three-year residency at Rockland State Hospital in Orangeburg, New York, before moving on to New York City, where she received Whirlwind's plea for assistance. She told Whirlwind that her stay in Lynchburg would be like serving purgatory on Earth. She would suffer, she said, but only for a short while.

Dr. El's presence made it easier for Whirlwind to concentrate on revitalizing his junior development program in the post-Ashe era. John Lucas, who became a top NBA player and coach, the Glass brothers (Sydney and Luis) and Linwood Simpson were among Whirlwind's most promising juniors. In an ironic twist on racial diversity, several white juniors, including Tina Watanabe of Los Angeles and "Rock" Devine, son of a Lynchburg physician also were in the program. "Some white people took notice of the miracles that he could perform; so they wanted their children to be a part of it," one of Whirlwind's relatives noted. Whirlwind reduced his travel time with the program, but maintained contact and control through several assistants. O.G. Walker, one of Whirlwind's longtime friends and associates, became his deputy commander. Walker took the team on most of the long trips: Kalamazoo, Chicago, etc. Ruth Langhorne, a Danville, Virginia, teacher, set aside the month of July each year to travel with the team and report back to Whirlwind. Hortense Creasy, Whirlwind's niece, stayed with him for several years and helped with chaperone and driving duties.

In 1965, when Ashe began his senior year at UCLA, Whirlwind's team was competing in more than 20 events per summer. Each year, the team played in at least one event that previously had been for whites only. Whirlwind seized every opportunity to break down racial barriers. In his 1965 annual ATA program he wrote, "This year we opened the doors to the Greensboro Junior Invitation, the Southern Girls (sic), the T.V.I., the last two of which are played in Chattanooga, Tennessee. We have played in the National 12 and 14 boys and girls (sic) in Chattanooga for a number of years. We have played in the Georgia State USLTA and the Volunteer State Junior Tournament at Vanderbilt University. Four brand new USLTA tournaments opened doors to our players. We either won or reached the finals in most of them. Our players have played sensational tennis!"

The success of Ashe and several other juniors who followed Ashe made Whirlwind a celebrity in the junior tennis world and the most influential person in black tennis. In March of 1966, he was named to the USLTA committee for the boys' and girls' 12 and 14 championships. A few months later, he received the prestigious Marlboro Award for his contributions to junior tennis. A feature article—accompanied by pictures of Whirlwind, Ashe and Gibson—on his achievements appeared in the October 1965 issue of *World Tennis* magazine. One of his most significant post-Ashe accomplishments, however, came in the form of a USLTA policy statement issued in 1969, two years after Dr. El answered his call for help.

The heading read: "Notice to All players applying for entry in USLTA Championships."

Then the statement: *"Associations holding tournaments, matches, competitions of ILTF meetings, shall guarantee that those accepted to compete or entitled to attend shall be allowed to do so.* In no circumstances shall there be racial discrimination.

"Teams or players whose entry has been accepted shall not withdraw except for reasons of health or bereavement or with the consent of the organizing committee, and any so doing shall have their entry refused for future tournaments, matches or competitions unless a written undertaking is given that such actions will not recur."

It was the USLTA's first policy statement specifically condemning the practice of racial discrimination at USLTA-sanctioned events. Long overdue, the statement in no small way was precipitated by Whirlwind's devotion and dedication to a program that many felt was doomed to fail. Dr. El was among Whirlwind's relatives, friends and admirers who praised him for his efforts.

"He lived for tennis," Dr. El said. "I am ashamed to admit it, but being a doctor was like a hobby. Tennis was his life."

Whirlwind, then close to 70, refused to rest on his laurels. He always kept busy, always seemed in a hurry to find and develop the next great black champion. Lo and behold, his search for greatness took him next door, where a 10-year-old swung his racket with the sureness and confidence of a promising master. In his aging heart, Whirlwind truly believed that Juan Farrow was only a few years—and maybe a million or so racket swings away—from stardom. His goal was to keep young Juan on track.

23

Juan

IN SOME WAYS, Whirlwind was the Nick Bollettieri of his time. Though he was never a standout on the tennis court, Whirlwind, like Bollettieri, was a master teacher and motivator, who had a gift for recognizing and grooming youngsters with superstar potential. Eventually, even white folks gave Whirlwind his due.

As founder of the ATA Junior Development Program and a member of the USLTA's committee for boys and girls in the 12 and 14 divisions in the late '60s, Whirlwind was one of the nation's most preeminent and influential coaches in junior tennis. Parents and coaches across the nation sought his counsel on matters involving the training and development of junior players.

People invariably asked him the same question: At what age should a child begin taking tennis lessons? Whirlwind generally responded with what became his standard answer: "When the child is interested and wants to play, the age should not be considered. If you have a tot you want to introduce to the wonderful world of tennis, don't worry about his age. The right time for him to start is NOW!"

To illustrate the point, Whirlwind would relate the case of the four-year-old tot who lived next door. Confined to his backyard, Juan Farrow spent hours watching Whirlwind teach older juniors on his backyard court. Juan never said a word to either the players or the elderly gentleman, who spent extra time with players slow to grasp the fundamentals. Then one day, Whirlwind, alone on the court, felt Juan's eyes tracking his movement.

JUAN

"He saw me watching and asked me if I wanted to come and be the ball boy, pick up balls for him," Juan said. "I said, 'Oh sure.' So he started showing me how to hold a racket, but instead of a real racket, he started me with a broom handle. I hit with that broom handle for—it had to be a good three months. He said, 'If you're able to hit a ball with a broom handle, then you'll be able to hit a ball in the middle of the strings with a racket.' After three months, he gave me a sawed-off short racket."

Whirlwind's reputation as the pied piper of juniors led wannabe tennis parents to stick short rackets or broomsticks into the hands of their toddlers. He described the techniques he used to teach those fresh from the cradle in a 1965 ATA program piece:

First, cut a broom handle the length of a tennis racket (about 27 inches). Then have the child stand in a batting stance like a baseball player with knees bent. Have him swing and at the same time, pivot, bending the front knee to get the weight behind the ball as a Willie Mays would do. In this way you teach the child the two basic and important things to remember: (1) Watch the ball and see it when you hit it, and (2) put your weight into the stroke.

Armed with the two fundamentals mentioned above, the child has the right foundation. When a child starts out playing without watching the ball, he develops into a 'ham' player because once reflex action becomes set in the direction of bad habits, like hitting the ball while watching the opponent, the child will never break the habits and become a superior player.

Whirlwind worked with young Juan and his brother, Paul, for the next few years. Occasionally, he'd take them to tournaments with the older players in his program. Though Juan was young and new to the game, Whirlwind never hesitated to emphasize his winning-is-everything philosophy.

"I was six or seven when I played in my first tournament," Juan said. "I got beat pretty bad. I remember Doc yelling at me a lot. Anytime I'd be losing, he would send my brother down to the court, and he'd say, 'Doc said if you don't win this match, he's not going to take you to the next tournament.' He tried to instill some kind of self-determination in you, more so than game technique. He was into teaching us to be strong mentally. He always urged us to have the will and guts to win, even when things were looking bad. I know it helped me a lot. I can't say it works for everybody. I'd be crying when I was losing, but when my brother came out, somehow I found a way to pull it out."

Juan's will to win, combined with his rare tenacity, made Whirlwind wonder if the boy next door would be the next black tennis superstar. Whirlwind raved about Juan to anyone within hearing range. He compared Juan to Ashe, adding quickly that he believed Juan was much better than Ashe at the same age, and predicted that Juan would be the youngest champion in every category. Whirlwind frequently discussed Juan's junior successes with Ashe, who was then a rising pro star. Whirlwind told Ashe that Juan had the skills, temperament and determination to follow in his footsteps on the pro tour. Ashe agreed. "Whenever Ashe was around, he'd practice with me and help me with my game," Juan said.

Wielding a flawless racket swing, Juan, like Ashe, followed Whirlwind's instructions unfailingly. When he was nine, even Juan felt stardom was a few hard years of work away.

"I first thought I could do it after I played in a 12-and-under tournament in Durham," Juan said. "Besides being just nine, I was the only black in the tournament and had to play the top seed in the first round. Doc was nervous, but I felt pretty good. I was pretty big for my age. Everybody used to think I was older than I was. Everybody crowded around my match and knew I was going to lose because I was playing the No. 1 seed. But I won 6-1, 6-0. And it was like, 'God! This is the No. 1 seed?' From then on, I just started doing well in the juniors. I felt I could play with these guys."

Mainly, Juan knew that Whirlwind would do everything necessary to keep him on course, as long as he adhered to Whirlwind's rules of order, which Juan summarized in two sentences: 'I'm the boss. Do it my way or not at all.' "

Juan had watched Whirlwind turn his back on several others, even family members, when they strayed from Whirlwind's my-way-or-the-highway philosophy. When he was five years old, Whirlwind's grandson, Bobby III, trained along with Juan during the summers in Lynchburg. Often, Juan sat quietly on Whirlwind's court watching grandfather and father argue about how Bobby III should be taught and who should teach him.

JUAN

"Doc was working with both of us because we were the youngest people he had," Juan said. "There were a few ups and downs when Big Bobby showed up because Big Bobby wanted to give his thoughts on what would help, and Doc would say, 'Hey, I'm the boss.' "

The conflict between Whirlwind and Bobby Jr. complicated Whirlwind's relationship with his grandson, especially since Juan showed far greater potential. "Dr. J knew he could do more for Juan than Bobby, but he had to keep peace in the family, too; so he had to give some attention to little Bobby," said Hortense Creasy, the daughter of Whirlwind's sister Victoria. "There was some jealousy."

Bobby III might have gone fishing and hunting with his grandfather once or twice, but their relationship was solidified on the tennis court. "It was all tennis," Bobby III said. "There was very little time for anything else. I might have started a couple of months before Juan. My grandfather stressed watching the ball; that was one of his cardinal rules. If you broke it, that was like committing a crime."

Juan and Bobby III often played doubles together in the 12-and-under division, but Bobby III wasn't a strong player. In the summer of 1970, Whirlwind paired Juan with Chip Hooper, a promising 12-year-old from Sunnydale, California. Chip's father, Dr. Lawrence Hooper, had learned of Whirlwind's program while living in Washington, D.C. Bobby Jr. was livid when he learned that his son would not be playing with Juan at the 12-and-under nationals in Chattanooga, Tennessee.

"I was violently angry when he did that to Little Bobby," Bobby Jr. said. "Little Bobby and Juan had played together quite a bit and had won two of their last three tournaments. I asked my father, 'How could you deny your own grandson a chance to win a national title?' He said he did because he thought Chip and Juan would have a better chance at winning the title, and he was probably right because they did win it."

Bobby III was aware of the strain that existed between his father and grandfather. He knew, too, that the rift had little to do with his grandfather substituting Hooper for him at the 12s doubles event in Tennessee. He knew it had more to do with his father's decision not to allow him to live with his grandfather.

"My grandfather took me to see Ashe and Marty Riessen play an exhibition match in Philadelphia," Bobby III said. "On the way back in the car, my grandfather said something about my father and school and about him wanting me to stay in Lynchburg year-round for as long as he could keep me. I don't remember this, but my father said that I told him at the time that if he didn't let me, my grandfather said the he wasn't going to send my father back to medical school. And that was it. That was the straw that broke the camel's back as far as my father was concerned. I continued to go to Lynchburg in the summer, but my father didn't go back to medical school."

Juan didn't allow the Johnson family feud to interfere with his development. He began his dominance of the 12-and-unders, defeating Eddie Reese of St. Petersburg, Florida, in the USLTA National 12-and-under final. In 1971, he was ranked No. 1 in the 12-and-under division. A year later, he stayed on course to fulfill Whirlwind's prediction by capturing the USLTA National 14-and-under title. The following year, he became No. 1 in the 14-and-under division.

Juan's dominance at the junior level occurred in the early '70s, just as pros were playing for large purses instead of large trophies. He became somewhat of a celebrity and often found himself pulled by one faction to play ATA events and by Whirlwind to play USLTA events. The lone black junior at USLTA events, at times, he was subjected to racial taunts and contempt. Some white parents who watched him play cheered when he made mistakes and rooted loudly for him to lose. "They couldn't stand to see their sons lose to Juan," Hortense Creasy said. "Some of them got really nasty."

Juan felt pressure—self-imposed and from others—to excel despite the obstacles.

Most talented youngsters learn to deal with the tensions and pressures tossed upon their young shoulders. Juan was among those who needed a crutch. He began smoking cigarettes at age 9 and discovered that they helped him relax. When he turned 12, he smoked nearly a-pack-a-day. "I was surprised that Dr. J never caught him," one of Juan's junior development teammates said. "When we'd go on trips, a lot of times he would smoke in his room before a match. Dr. J would go in, just before Juan would put the cigarette out, but Doc never noticed or just didn't say anything."

Juan was a major force in USLTA competition throughout his junior career. Juan beat Hall of Famer John McEnroe and several other former pros—Eliot Teltscher, Mel Purcell, Chip Hooper and John Sadri—in junior competition. "I beat McEnroe in 1977, about four weeks before he reached the Wimbledon semifinals," Juan said. "That also was the last time I played him."

Though Whirlwind didn't oversee Juan's practice sessions or wasn't at courtside during the years he beat top 18s juniors, including McEnroe, Juan continued to carry Whirlwind's teachings and game plan in his heart. "He wouldn't allow us to throw rackets or cuss, but he would always be on the sidelines doing all the yelling and screaming for us," Juan said. "I guess the thing that he most instilled in me was to keep your cool at all times. I feel that has been a trademark of all the people who have ever been under his wings. Whether they made it or not, all have been cool on the court."

24

Last Reward

E. T. (TEDDY) PENZOLD and Papa Jerry, two of Whirlwind's special heroes, stole away home in 1970.

Penzold, the USLTA official who helped Whirlwind integrate the Interscholastic Championships in Charlottesville in 1951, died in June 1970. Despite strong opposition from Charlottesville USLTA officials, Penzold had stood his ground and adamantly maintained that blacks be allowed to play in the national event for high school players. Colgate Darden, president of the University of Virginia at the time, supported Penzold's unpopular stance, thus allowing Whirlwind to continue the pursuit of what many of his colleagues considered an impossible dream.

The soft-spoken Penzold also had encouraged Whirlwind to organize a national black interscholastic championship to expand his search for black talent. Whirlwind and Teddy shared a friendship rooted in mutual respect and admiration. Theirs was a bond that rarely gelled in a society that was steeped in color consciousness. "Dr. Johnson sent me a wonderful bouquet and a long letter at the time my husband died," Lucy Penzold said. "In the letter, he said the flowers were from all the members of his junior development program."

Papa Jerry, who was 90 when he died in May 1970, was buried next to Mama Nancy in Plymouth. Whirlwind sat next to his sister Eva at Papa Jerry's funeral. Oblivious to those around him, Whirlwind spent several minutes in an animated conversation with his deceased parents. "It was very strange," Eva said.

LAST REWARD

"Mama, I thought I was going to die first and be buried next to you," Whirlwind said, "but Papa Jerry beat me to it. I'll be next."

Eva nudged him. "Shhh," she said.

"Okay, I'll be nice. But Papa, I'm going to be buried next to you."

"Shh," Eva said, nudging him again.

After the funeral, Eva revisted this idea of Whirlwind being buried in Plymouth.

"Robert, aren't you going to be buried in Lynchburg?" she asked, thinking he would want to be buried in Lynchburg. Since he had lived there so long.

"No," he said, "I want to be buried with Mama and Papa."

Eva: "I told him that Waltee was set on having his funeral in Lynchburg and that he'd better discuss it with Waltee and Bobby Jr. if he wanted his body brought back to Plymouth. Sure enough, that same day, he sat down with Waltee and Bobby Jr. and told them what he wanted. Waltee said, 'No, no, you have to be buried in Lynchburg.' When he went back to Lynchburg after Papa Jerry's funeral, he had it written in his will that his body would be brought back to Plymouth."

The deaths of Penzold and Papa Jerry prompted Whirlwind to contemplate his own mortality. A month after celebrating his 71st birthday, Whirlwind realized that he had moved through life at breakneck speed during the past 20 years. His office hours often were frantic and most of his weekends passed in a blur. At times, he'd motor as far as Florida or as near as Richmond, always with a group of his juniors in tow. Once the weekend ended, he always hurried back home to Lynchburg.

"He used to always tell us to be ready to leave in time for him to make office hours Monday morning," said Hortense Creasy, Whirlwind's niece, who acted as his chauffeur on those weekend trips during the '60s when Whirlwind first began slowing down a bit . . . "Even when we went to Florida for the Orange Bowl junior tournament, we left in time for him to get back to make office hours. You know, he never liked the idea of people passing him on the highway, even when he wasn't driving. When he saw a car passing us, he would say, 'Look, too many people are passing us. Go faster!' "

Throughout his adult life, Whirlwind functioned with computer-like efficiency, seemingly without very much time reserved for preventive maintenance. "Sometimes, when he would be traveling, he would say, 'Just give me five minutes and I'll be okay,' " Hortense said. "And he would go right to sleep just like that. I could never do that. I'd always toss and turn. But with him, five minutes later, he would be up and ready to drive. Dr. J had a lot of energy."

Some of Whirlwind's weekend junkets were strictly pleasure trips, escapes from the rigors of his life as a physician. Some weekends, he would leave Lynchburg on Fridays at 9:30 p.m. and drive to Wilmington, North Carolina, getting there about midnight. Then he'd play poker until 4 a.m., go to bed, wake up around 8 a.m. and play tennis all day long. Then he would shower, eat and drive back to Lynchburg in time for work on Monday morning.

Bobby Jr. was among the few who knew Whirlwind's secret for such incredible stamina:

One time, in 1955, we were playing in a father-son doubles match in Cleveland. We lost and went back to our hotel room. He sat down and started writing, sending out press releases, letters asking for money for the program and a thousand other things. There was a bottle of liquor on the table. We both started tasting and got real high.

The next day, we were scheduled to leave for St. Louis to defend our previous year's championship. He wouldn't let me drive. He said, 'You sleep, you'll have to carry me tomorrow.' I couldn't have slept even if I had wanted to. I found out the next day that he had taken some pills to keep him awake.

We played a terrible match. He was missing everything that came at him. I couldn't figure out what was wrong. The ball would go past him and then he would dive after it. His eyes had a strange look in them. It was the first time in my life that I wanted to quit a tennis match. We lost, but later, he told me he had taken some pills to make him sleep because he was so hopped up from the other pills. He never told me how tired he was. He was 56 then and had been rolling like that for years."

But when Whirlwind passed the 70-year mark, some of his systems slipped out of sync. His body—which had served him well while he created the "legend of Whirlwind" on the gridiron at Lincoln, knocked down racial barriers in junior tennis, collected college degrees, and chased women and tennis balls during his peripatetic life—finally sagged from wear and tear.

LAST REWARD

"Dr. J was never sick until August 1970," his companion, Erdice Creasy, said. "He got sick while attending an Omega Psi Phi conference in Pittsburgh. He came back home after two days of a weeklong meeting. A friend of his, Carl Hutcherson, went with him. Carl worried me to death about Dr. J. He thought that was the end."

With a bit of rest at home, Whirlwind survived that illness, but three months later, after returning from a hunting trip before Thanksgiving, he again became seriously ill.

"He spat up an awful lot of blood," Erdice said. "We took him to the Lynchburg General Hospital. In January, he went to Duke University for tests. In March, he called the people at Duke and asked when he could return there for surgery because he was getting worse."

Said Dr. William Massie, a Lynchburg physician, "He had lost some weight, had not felt well and had vomited some blood. We tried to find out why he had bled from the esophagus. The pressure had built up in the esophagus because of scarring in the liver. He was received at Duke and they did an operation there which relieved the pressure some."

Whirlwind was bedridden for weeks after returning home from the operation. Pain was an unwelcome companion. "He had never said anything about having pain until after the surgery," Erdice said. "He wanted injections, but Dr. El told me not to give him too many."

Whirlwind protested, "I'm the one suffering!"

Said Erdice, "Dr. J used to say that he felt he was doing his job as long as he could keep his patients comfortable and without pain. He didn't want to see them suffering. I guess that's the way he felt about himself."

Dr. Eaton, Whirlwind's longtime colleague from Wilmington, refused to let him lay in bed feeling alone and helpless, reminding him that, as a doctor, he knew a patient shouldn't stay in bed any longer than necessary.

"You've got to get up, man," Eaton told him, having spent an entire afternoon in Lynchburg trying to encourage Whirlwind.

"Well, I feel weak," Whirlwind said.

"Hell, I'll help you," said Eaton, tugging his friend out of the bed.

Despite an oppressive schedule, Whirlwind faithfully attended commencement exercises and class reunions at Lincoln as often as possible.

WHIRLWIND

Several of his college classmates kept in touch with him over the years and were especially attentive during his illness. Lincoln was his heart as much as Plymouth was his home. When word of his grave condition reached Lincoln administrators, plans to recognize a favorite son were expedited. "Lincoln was going to present him with an honorary doctorate at the commencement exercises in June 1971, but they weren't sure he was going to make it," Erdice said. "So they arranged to present it to him in Lynchburg on May 23rd.

"Oh, if only I could just make it until the 23rd of May," Whirlwind said.

Said Erdice, "That's all he wanted to do. Of course, he loved Lincoln like it was a human being."

Lincoln president Dr. Herman Branson and classmates James McCrae and Wayman Costen presented the doctorate to Whirlwind in Lynchburg. A few weeks later, Whirlwind went to Lincoln for the commencement exercises. He walked across the stage and again received the degree, this time in cap and gown. Erdice, Whirlwind's sister Dr. El and his son, Bobby Jr., accompanied him.

Dr. George Cannon, one of Whirlwind's classmates and a generous contributor to the ATA Junior Development Program, kept members of Lincoln's class of '24 informed of alumni whereabouts and professional achievements. "We had a good class," Cannon said. "We kept together. Every five years, we'd have a reunion. As we got older, the motto of our class was 'Keep breathing.' I got a note from Whirlwind after he received his honorary degree. It said, 'George, it's getting hard to breath.' Three days later, he died."

On the last Sunday morning of his life, Whirlwind had cantaloupe with strawberries and blueberries for breakfast. He ate only half of the cantaloupe, put the rest in the refrigerator and told Erdice he would finish it after attending services at Diamond Hill Baptist Church. The weather was warm and sunny on June 28, 1971, very much like that wondrous day in June 1951 when Whirlwind took Victor Miller and Roosevelt Megginson to Charlottesville to become the first blacks to play in the USLTA National Interscholastic Championships. He had hoped to take Juan Farrow, then 13, to the event, which had been moved to Massachusetts. Whirlwind felt in his bones that Juan would achieve as much as—if not more than—Ashe had achieved. For a while that morning, Whirlwind shoved aside his own aches and pain when he learned that Juan was injured.

"I was going to take Juan to play in a tournament in Durham the next day, but something was wrong with his arm," Erdice said. "So Dr. J wanted Juan to see the doctor before I took him to church. While we were waiting for Juan at the doctor's office, Dr. J said he would like to go to Plymouth to go fishing, but he didn't have a way of getting there. I told him that since I had to take Juan to Durham I could drive him to Plymouth first. So that was no problem. He said, 'Oh yeah, that would be fine.'

"When I let him out at the church, I asked him what time he wanted me to pick him up. He said. 'That's okay. El and Sister Victoria will be there; so I'll get a ride back with them.' I think I was the last one to talk to him."

Whirlwind, once inside the church, sat down and collapsed shortly before Dr. El and Sister Victoria arrived. "Somebody ran up to the car and said something to El," Victoria said. "They never want me to face anything; so they pushed me back. El told me she had to go to the hospital with Dr. J. The usher in the church said when he saw Whirlwind, he was putting something in his mouth."

An ambulance rushed Whirlwind to Lynchburg General Hospital, but he never regained consciousness. "We did an emergency operation on him, but he was bleeding into the abdomen itself from a tumor of the liver," Dr. Massie said. "That's what caused his death. It was not diagnosed until that time. Nobody knew he had the malignancy. He died rather quickly."

Dr. Massie, who had cared for Whirlwind throughout his illness, treated him at home when he was too weak to make the trip to his office. "As sick as he was, he apologized to Dr. Massie for keeping him up nights," Dr. El said. "He was polite and gentle even when he was ill."

Dr. Massie admired Whirlwind as much as a patient as he did as a colleague. "He was a very remarkable, self-controlled uncomplaining patient," Massie said. "He was very easy to take care of. In the relationship with my staff and me, he was very quiet. He didn't make a big deal of things. He kept a lot in."

25

Ten Feet Tall

Baptized as a little boy in the Roanoke River near his North Carolina home, Whirlwind grew up praising the word of God at Plymouth's New Chapel Baptist Church. Shortly after settling in Lynchburg, he joined the Diamond Hill Baptist Church. On the final Sunday of June 1971, the day he died, Whirlwind had sat in a pew of that church shortly before slipping into a state of unconsciousness from which he never recovered.

A tribute to Whirlwind in the funeral program included these observations:

It is, no doubt, significantly symbolic that his last footsteps were taken on the premises of his church. Neither blaring trumpets nor rolling drums proclaimed his faith, but it came alive in innumerable acts of Christian charity and concern for his fellow man. He had the ability to motivate and inspire others to strive for excellence. Into the infinite compassion of God do we immerse our own deep sense of loss and look confidently to the dawn of that new day when Dr. R. Walter Johnson and all who sleep in Him shall awake in a new world and to a day that is everlasting.

Funeral services for Robert Walter Johnson were held the following Thursday at the Court Street Baptist Church. Diamond Hill was considered too small to hold those expected to pay their last respects to one of Lynchburg's most distinguished citizens. But even Court Street church, with a seating capacity of 350, wasn't large enough to accommodate Whirlwind's throng of mourners. With no seats available inside, more than 100 people stood outside in the warm sunshine, straining to hear hymns and eulogies rendered to commemorate the life and times of one of black America's many unsung heroes. Cars with license plates from as far as New York, Connecticut and New Jersey brought classmates and friends to bid farewell to the man they affectionately called "Whirlwind." His obituary appeared in newspapers and magazines throughout the country.

Rev. Haywood Robinson Jr., the Diamond Hill minister, presided from the pulpit. Rev. James Brooks, the Court Street minister, gave the invocation. Rev. Herman Ford, the Rivermont Baptist Church minister, read passages from the Bible and Elder Fletcher Hubbard, minister of True Holiness Church, offered a prayer of comfort.

The Diamond Hill Baptist Church choir sang *"I Heard the Voice of Jesus Say"* and *"A Mighty Fortress Is Our God."* Marcia Allar, who worked in Whirlwind's office, sang *"How Great Thou Art."* Responding to a special request from Bobby Jr., choir member Hiawatha Johnson (not related) gave a soulful rendition of Frank Sinatra's *"My Way."* With penetrating power and emotion, Johnson spiced each verse with a touch of gospel and made several mourners feel that he, indeed, had walked more than a few miles in Whirlwind's moccasins. "It was a song that was more or less his way of life," Johnson said.

C. W. Seay, a member of the Lynchburg City Council, spoke of Whirlwind's contributions to the city as a physician, civic leader and activist. Dr. Hubert Eaton, who represented the American Tennis Association, spoke of Robert's love of tennis and his lifelong commitment to developing young black players. Several of his tennis protégés—the famous and not-so-famous—were in the audience.

Althea Gibson, who had looked upon Whirlwind as a father and was inducted into the International Tennis Hall of Fame a few weeks after his death, was there. Juan Farrow, who at the time was ranked No. 1 in the nation in the 12-and-under category, was there. But Arthur Ashe, groomed and nurtured by Whirlwind throughout his teenage years, was conspicuous by his absence. Several of Whirlwind's family members, including Waltee and Bobby Jr., were deeply distressed by Ashe's failure to attend the funeral. They said that Ashe's decision to stay to compete in the Wimbledon doubles was not an acceptable excuse. "Answer me this," a niece said. "If it had been Donald Dell or Andy Young who had died, would he have left Wimbledon to attend their funeral?"

Whirlwind was buried on the first Thursday of the Wimbledon fortnight. Ashe lost to Marty Riessen in the third round of singles before Whirlwind's death. Ashe and partner Dennis Ralston were still alive in the doubles competition. Ashe said he based his decision to stay on his belief that Whirlwind would have wanted him to stay and compete in the doubles. He noted further that he abhorred funerals and didn't attend his mother's funeral when she died. He was six years old at the time. In the early 1980s, when discussing his absence from Whirlwind's funeral, Ashe said that he had attended only three funerals—a grandfather and both grandmothers—in his lifetime.

Waltee and Bobby Jr. had grown up together watching their father devote more time to other children—especially Ashe—than his own children. At times, they felt that their father seemed more concerned about the growth of some of the other children—especially Ashe—than he did about their growth. Neither Waltee nor Bobby Jr. accepted Ashe's rationale for skipping their father's funeral.

"Arthur Ashe couldn't have known how much my father loved him," Waltee said. "If he did, he wouldn't have missed his funeral. I think daddy would have wanted him to be there."

In a voice singed with anger, Bobby Jr. said, "Nobody likes to go to funerals. The thing that annoyed me about Ashe's position is that I feel Dr. J would have wanted him there. If you could ask him, he may have said, 'No, it's not important.' But I think he would have wanted it and I think he deserved it. My father literally picked this boy up from nothing and made him what he is today."

The presence of two women, Nona Johnson Reid and Olivia (pseudonym), known to be Whirlwind's out-of-wedlock daughters, proved to be even more unsettling to Waltee and Bobby Jr. than Ashe's absence. Nona Johnson Reid was born in Plymouth when Whirlwind was 17. At the time, Nona's mother insisted that Whirlwind was the child's father, but Whirlwind maintained that he wasn't. Despite Whirlwind's denials, Papa Jerry and Mama Nancy accepted Nona as their granddaughter and helped her mother raise her. Mama Nancy's rationale was that the child should not be made to suffer because of the questionable circumstances of her birth.

When Nona became an adult, she changed her name to Johnson and became involved with family gatherings. Whenever Whirlwind showed up in Plymouth on fishing or hunting trips, Nona visited him. She once redecorated his room at his parents' home. She visited Whirlwind during his illness and, to Whirlwind's dismay, fussed over his care. "One day, he said, 'Please do something to get her out of my hair,' " a relative said. "I told him, 'Well, I didn't put her in your hair.' " Some family members didn't want to describe Nona as one of Whirlwind's surviving daughters, but she made it clear that she wouldn't accept anything less than full disclosure. Nona prevailed on that issue.

Waltee grudgingly sanctioned Nona's request, but cringed at the thought of having, Olivia, Whirlwind's other out-of-wedlock daughter, also listed as a surviving daughter. "Waltee asked me not to have my name put on the program," Olivia said. "My mother would have had a fit anyway. He really wanted everybody to know I was his daughter, but my mother wouldn't let me tell everybody. I didn't see any sense in upsetting Waltee; so I didn't have my name put on the program. What good would it have done? He was already gone."

But not forgotten.

Whirlwind lived on through his players and family members. Arthur Ashe, who later won Wimbledon (1975) stayed near the top of the pro rankings during most of the 1970s. Juan Farrow became one of the top juniors in the country in each age division before turning pro. Dr. El, Whirlwind's sister, continued to operate a health clinic that mainly serviced Lynchburg's black population. Dr. El wanted desperately to leave Lynchburg after her brother died, but she couldn't ignore his pleas, whispered at a time when she knew he was near death. "He said, 'Please, don't leave,' " said Dr. El more than 10 years after her brother's death. "He begged me to stay and take care of his patients. He was very sick. How could I leave?

"And you know, there's not a day that goes by that at least one of his patients won't say something about him. Some of them will say, 'You ain't like your brother; your brother would have taken these tonsils out right here.' Or, 'Your brother wouldn't have done that.' It irks me sometimes. They really loved him and he was a blessing for Lynchburg."

Twelve years after his death, the name plate next to the front door of his brown and white house still read: "Dr. R. Walter Johnson." He was still listed in the Lynchburg telephone book. Erdice Creasy, then 73, the woman who had become Whirlwind's most trusted employee, closest friend and companion in his later years, lived alone in the house. In his will, Whirlwind specified that Erdice and Eva Cooper, his sister, be given life-long rights to the two-story house. Erdice said that upon her death the house would belong to Whirlwind's three grandsons.

"It's not really that big," she said in the summer of 1982. "The attic is used to store furniture and the basement is cluttered and not used anymore. I just use the three rooms on the first floor and two on the second."

The house, Erdice said, was decorated mostly with memories of the life she had shared with the man who was the most important force in her adult life. Her continued presence there, quite likely was her way of telling the world what most of black Lynchburg already knew: that although they never married, she was the special woman in Whirlwind's life and that he didn't forget all that she had meant to him. Among other things, Whirlwind left her a lump sum of $1,000 and a yearly allotment of $1,920.

Erdice wore two diamond rings, both given to her by Whirlwind. She wore one ring, which had a round stone, on a finger on her right hand; she wore the other, which was oval-shaped, on her left hand, on the finger where the wedding band customarily is worn. "I think as a whole, over all the years, I knew Dr. J. better than his wife (Peggy) did," Erdice said. "I don't think anybody else would put up with him as a husband. That's true. He was an unusual type person. I mean, sort of domineering. You couldn't say nothing to him about what he wanted to do."

She spoke softly and lovingly of the life she shared with Whirlwind, reflecting evenly on his strengths and weaknesses, likes and dislikes. "He drank bourbon and beer sometimes," Erdice said. "He didn't smoke. He tried to smoke a cigar once, but had to put it down. Papa Jerry smoked cigars. He didn't use swear words, but he would say 'damn' and 'hell,' something like that. He used to use the expression, 'that old bastard,' sometimes.

"He loved watermelon. He'd always put a half of watermelon in the refrigerator in his office, and he'd put the other half upstairs in my apartment. Before he'd do anything or see any patients, he'd say 'Why don't you cut me a piece of fruit.' He didn't want the patients to hear him say watermelon, so he'd call it fruit. I used to tell him, 'You might as well say it, because they can smell it all over the place.' He'd eat that piece of watermelon and come home at night and take another piece from my refrigerator."

Erdice remembered seeing sheer joy in his eyes the day Ashe won the 1968 U.S. Open title. "Dr. J was so happy over that he didn't know what to do." She recalled, too, an all-consuming sadness that dominated his mood throughout the time that he and Bobby Jr. argued about Little Bobby living in Lynchburg and Bobby Jr. not returning to medical school. "Dr. J was so disappointed."

Her relationship with Whirlwind grew stronger as they grew older. When Dr. El moved to Lynchburg to help with his practice, Erdice became Whirlwind's regular traveling partner on social trips. "We'd go to the Penn Relays; I used to like that," she said. "And we'd go to see the Redskins play in Washington. He had season tickets. We went to New York to Forest Hills for the tennis matches every year, too. The only time we'd go to a movie was when we were in New York. I think the last movie we saw together was the Martin Luther King story." On his birthday, Erdice would accompany him to Plymouth for his annual celebration with Papa Jerry. "We'd always go fishing while we were there," she said. "You know he hunted a lot, too. If he got out of a car, he wouldn't want to have to walk a block, but he would walk for days to hunt. He really loved the outdoors."

Outside, the backyard clay court, where Ashe and a generation of black juniors slapped tennis balls back and forth, had become a breeding ground for weeds. Some members of the Lynchburg Tennis Association had discussed with some of Whirlwind's relatives the possibility of restoring the court and operating a junior program in his memory. The plan was abandoned, however, mainly because Erdice's presence made it impossible for family members to guarantee that the association would have easy access and control.

There were talks, too, of turning the house into a historical site. The Anne Spencer House, which is in the 1300 block on Pierce Street, about 200 yards from Whirlwind's home, became a historical site shortly after Spencer, a black poet, died. A historical marker on the sidewalk in front of the house reads: *This was the house of Edward Alexander and Anne Bannister Spencer from 1903 until her death on July 25, 1975. Born on Feb. 6, 1862 in Henry County, Virginia, Anne Spencer was to receive national and international recognition as a poet. Published extensively between 1920 and 1935, she belonged to the Harlem Renaissance School of Writers.*

Those close to Whirlwind said deep down, indeed, he might have yearned for greater recognition and respect. But essentially, his goals were more a rejection of white America's bid to make black Americans believe their tales of black inferiority than they were about self-aggrandizement. Like most educated black men of his era, Whirlwind's goal was to help the next generation of blacks circumvent the racial barriers created to rob them of, among other things, a strong sense of self worth. Like Whirlwind, black teachers—foot soldiers among the black elite at the time—understood the impact racism was having in black classrooms. Though they couldn't guarantee a brighter future, black teachers assured their students that a more satisfying life awaited those who strove to be twice as good, twice as smart as any white youngster. It was an unrealistic goal presented in the reality of an unfair and often cruel existence. But unrealistic goals can be reached, as Whirlwind proved.

Many of his contemporaries saw Whirlwind's dream of watching a black junior capture the USLTA Interscholastic Singles Championship as an unreachable goal. But Whirlwind lived to see Arthur Ashe reach that goal and much more.

The day after his funeral, Whirlwind's body was taken to Plymouth for burial, keeping the promise he had made at his father's gravesite. A caravan of more than 100 cars made the five-hour drive from Lynchburg to Plymouth. Whirlwind was laid to rest in a plot next to his parents in Toodle Cemetery. Most of his lifetime contributions are inscribed on the face of his tombstone. The inscription reads:

TEN FEET TALL

- *Lincoln University Alumni Award—1964*
- *Doctor of Humane Letters Award—1971*
- *He obtained more than one hundred scholarships for players.*
- *He won 55 trophies in tennis including six national championships.*
- *Founder of the American Tennis Association's Junior Development Program.*
- *Coached Althea Gibson, Arthur Ashe Jr., Juan Farrow*
- *Marlboro Tennis Award*
- *Omega Psi Phi Fraternity Award*
- *NAACP Life Membership Chairman*
- *Spiro T. Agnew Honorary Citizenship Award*
- *Integrated Lynchburg General Hospital Staff*

His Living Was Not in Vain

The tombstone that marks the final resting place of Robert Walter Johnson towers above all the other markers in the cemetery. It is, in fact, nearly 10 feet tall.

Epilogue

IN HIS LAST WILL AND TESTAMENT, Whirlwind divided his worldly possessions among family and friends. From an estate valued at close to $120,000, he left lump sums, ranging from $250 to $1,000. His out-of-wedlock daughters, Olivia and Nona, also received monetary gifts.

Personal items that Whirlwind treasured went to friends he believed would treasure them, too. George Hamlet of Brookneal, Virginia, received his 12- and 16-gauge automatic guns and all his beagle hounds and bird dogs. Joe Pruden of Plymouth, North Carolina, received three outboard motors. Walter Coleman of Lynchburg got a double-barrel shotgun. Gracie Hilton of Gladstone, Virginia, got a hunting dog and $250. Family members received the bulk of the estate, which included nine properties, but the soft-spoken physician also left something of value to hundreds of the youngsters he helped during a generation of generosity.

When I reflect on my brief stay under Whirlwind's wing and listen still to the tales of many of my contemporaries whose lives also were shaped by his touch, I'm smothered with fond memories of the man who was, in my mind, the Godfather of Black Tennis. No one else cast a more paternal eye on his juniors or came close to matching his commitment, guile and determination. His efforts were not in vain.

Some who learned the nuances of the game and life lessons from Whirlwind later spent countless hours reciting his teachings to the next generation of talented black juniors. Indeed, some of today's aspiring black juniors continue to be motivated and inspired by Whirlwind's disciples.

Willis Thomas, Ashe's 12-and-under doubles partner, says, "I was blessed to coach several top-ranked pros, including Zina Garrison, Lori McNeil, Rodney Harmon and Katrina Adams, and it still warms my heart when they tell me that they passed on to youngsters some of the things that they learned from me. What they're doing mostly is passing on the things I learned from Whirlwind and it makes me proud to know that a piece of Whirlwind is still being passed on to others."

Thomas continues to follow Whirlwind's example as a tennis administrator/coach for the Washington Tennis & Education Foundation, which provides many inner-city youths with tennis and educational training. Bobby Davis, Arthur Carrington, Beverly Coleman and several others followed in Whirlwind's footsteps by establishing tennis academies. Carrington, a former ATA champion, owns an academy in Amherst, Massachusetts. Davis headed an academy in upstate New York before moving to Bradenton, Florida, to work at Nick Bollettieri's academy. He now runs a recreational tennis center in Bradenton.

"Dr. J showed us what could happen if we could get a critical mass of talented kids to train in the same place," Davis said. "He knew we would all become better because we would feed off each other. That's what I try to do with my program, and that's the exact philosophy that Nick Bollettieri uses at his academy. Of course, Nick has a lot of money available for his program, whereas Dr. J. had to continue to practice medicine in order to provide for us."

Former pro Leslie Allen, who reached a career high No. 17 in 1981, is the executive director of a foundation that carries her name. The foundation's goal, says Allen, who was 10 when she trained at Whirlwind's home, is to introduce young African Americans to tennis and to career opportunities in tennis-related businesses, including sports promotion, management, marketing and journalism. Allen says the foundation's motto, "Tennis is more than just hitting the ball," epitomizes Whirlwind's teaching approach, on and off the court.

"I tell my kids that when they're 13 or 14 and realize that they might not be good enough to be superstars, I want them to know that there is a whole wealth of opportunities behind the scenes in tennis that I have

EPILOGUE

access to and they can have access to," Allen says. "The main thing I took away from the Dr. J experience was the importance of developing a strong sense of responsibility that you have to have to be a top-ranked player. Basically, I tell them, 'You've got to have your shit together. You've got to learn how to speak to people, know how to dress, know how to be on time, know how to write and have a sense of tennis history so that you'll know what other people have gone through, so you won't think that what you're doing is so tough.' It's been very rewarding to see the kids get it."

In the late '70s, Whirlwind's impact as a benefactor and sports trailblazer became more widely acknowledged. A more diverse tennis community saw merit in Whirlwind's struggle to overcome the racial bias of that time. His cause, of course, was boosted by persistent accolades from his primary protégés: Ashe, who died in 1993, and Gibson, who died in 2003. Both often said that they would not have become the first African Americans to win Grand Slam tournament titles without Whirlwind. Some Whirlwind juniors received collegiate athletic scholarships and others found employment as tennis instructors/coaches at various tennis academies/public parks.

For more than 20 consecutive years, until his death in 1971, groups of black youngsters spent expense-free summers training at his home. Whirlwind's death confirmed what many of that era already knew: without Whirlwind, the ATA Junior Development Program, based at his home, wouldn't last. A Lynchburg sports group recently asked city officials to preserve Whirlwind's Pierce Street home as a historical site.

I can't say that my early exposure to the Lynchburg physician prompted me to make tennis my racket, career-wise. But I can say that at times I felt the spirit of Whirlwind guiding my thoughts as I chronicled the exploits of his prized pupils, Althea and Arthur. During a 30-year newspaper career, which included 15 as *USA Today's* tennis writer, I covered the pros from courtside seats in the world's major tennis arenas. My journalism career, which began at New York's *Newsday* in 1970, brought me back in contact with Arthur, who by then had become a tennis superstar. We saw each other more often when his health forced him off the court and into media rooms as a sports journalist. We chatted often about anything and everything, including the sparse number of

African Americans on the men and women's pro circuits. The number of African Americans competing on the major pro tours remains disproportionately low.

Since the Open era began, less than a dozen African-American men and a bit more than a dozen women have been ranked in the Top 200 of the ATP and WTA tours. Sisters Venus and Serena Williams were among the best of about a half-dozen black women to finish 2003 ranked on the WTA Tour, and James Blake has been the lone African-American male in the Top 100 on the ATP since 2001. Thus far, Venus and Serena have been the only African-American pros to join Gibson and Ashe as Grand Slam tournament singles champions. Zina Garrison (1990 Wimbledon finalist) and MaliVai Washington (1996 Wimbledon finalist) came close to making Grand Slam breakthroughs at Wimbledon.

Rodney Harmon, a former pro who was appointed the USTA's director of men's tennis in 2001, is confident that a cadre of promising young African-American juniors soon will be among the next wave of top U.S. juniors to join the pro tours. The 2003 season ended with James Blake, ranked No. 37, the only black in the Top 200. Blake's older brother, Thomas, No. 436, was the next highest-ranked African-American pro. Harmon, who in 1982 joined Ashe as the only African American men to reach the U.S. Open quarterfinal, says James Blake's status as the lone top-ranked black is a rarity that he hopes to rectify.

"For the last three years, the No. 1 ranked player in the boys 14s has been African American," Harmon says. "In 2001, Timothy Neilly was the nation's top-ranked junior in the 14s. In 2002, Marcus Fugate was the world's No. 1 ranked junior, and in 2003, Donald Young (was) No. 1 in the world in the 14s. (In Dec. 2003, Young became the first African American to win a singles title in the 57-year history of the Orange Bowl International Championships played in Key Biscayne. Young defeated Germany's Aljoscho Thron 3-6, 6-3, 6-2 in the final.)

"If they can be No. 1 in the world at 14, they're talented enough to be No. 1 in the world at 17 and to be top-ranked pros. We're trying to help them improve their games, get stronger faster and play in pro events. I'm hoping that we'll have a long, continuous train of really good players so that there's not a break in the action like there has been the past few years.

"Obviously, African Americans in the sport face different issues, and if those issues aren't addressed, then they will never be able to become successful on the tour because they can't adapt to all the changes on the tour. What we're doing is addressing the issues early on, talking through the problems. There are a lot of problems they face that don't get addressed. But as talented as these guys are, if we don't get them to the highest level, I've definitely made some errors."

A Richmond, Virginia, native, Harmon was coached during his junior years by Thomas. At times, he traveled and trained with Garrison and McNeil when they were coached by Thomas and John Wilkerson. Though Harmon never met Whirlwind, he sensed his influence and wisdom through his dealings with Ashe and Thomas.

"He died just a few years before I would have gone to his training camp in Lynchburg," Harmon says. "Everyone in the ATA talked about him so much. I knew Willis had gone to his camp and how he stressed discipline, and I knew all about what he had done for Arthur and Juan Farrow. I found all the things he had done so interesting."

Like many other ATA followers, I believed Arthur's victories at the 1968 U.S. Open and 1975 Wimbledon would inspire scores of young, gifted black athletes to strive to become tennis champions. A few did, but for the most part, the blue chip athletes of color stayed with the less expensive and more accessible team sports: basketball, football and baseball. Part of the problem, Ashe said in a story I wrote for *USA Today* in 1991, was that the white tennis community often failed to provide black juniors with the proper training and emotional support needed because it feared that black athletes would dominate tennis as they do basketball.

"I absolutely think that," Ashe said. "I hear it all the time from other blacks. Big-time tennis is viewed by minorities as inhospitable. I am not saying it's true, but it comes as a result of a feeling of a lack of acceptance. You're viewed as an outsider, like, 'We'll tolerate just a few of you.' They are afraid that we'll get a toehold and we'll take it over. The orientation of officers of the USTA is definitely toward private clubs."

Bob Cookson, the USTA president at the time, vehemently denied

Ashe's charge that the organization feared a black takeover. "That's absurd," Cookson said. "I have never head that from anyone in the USTA."

Arthur held his ground on the issue and cited U.S. tennis officials' unwillingness to keep Gibson in the game by providing her with a job as an example of their indifference toward black achievers.

"As good as she was, she was the only great U.S. champion I know who had financial problems," Ashe said. "If she were white, there's no question she would have been helped."

Arthur pointed to the USTA's failure to add John Wilkerson to its junior development coaching staff as another example of the organization's failure to pursue black achievers.

"I don't know of any other teaching pro who has taken two women (Garrison and McNeil) to Top 10 status," Arthur said. "If Wilkerson were white, he would have been swamped with job offers."

Garrison and McNeil broke into the Top 10 of the WTA Tour in the mid-'80s. In the late 1990s, the Williams sisters, coached by their parents, Richard Williams and Oracene Price, established themselves as the women's tour's dominant pros. Chip Hooper, Katrina Adams, Marcel Freeman, Chanda Rubin, Todd Nelson, Bryan Shelton and Leslie Allen are among less than three dozen U.S.-born blacks to compete on the pro tours since 1968. (See Appendix A & B for complete list.).

Arthur unquestionably worked diligently to draw talented blacks to the game, especially after he retired. Several of his former protégés doubted that he had his heart in it while he was an active pro.

Luis Glass, Horace Reid, Arthur Carrington and Juan Farrow were among the rising young black stars who sought and received guidance and assistance from Arthur shortly after Whirlwind died. Each, for different reasons, fell short of becoming top pros. And each, in varying degrees, blamed Arthur for their failures.

Based on Arthur's recommendations, Glass, the 1960 ATA boys' 12 champion, and Reid, the 1972 ATA men's champion, received scholarships to Arthur's alma mater, UCLA. Social problems cut short Glass' stay there; Reid was forced to leave after losing his scholarship. Arthur sent Glass to Hampton University in Hampton, Virginia, where he stayed for two years before losing his scholarship because of behavior problems. Arthur attempted to send Reid to Hampton, believing his chances of improving his game would be better at Hampton than in California. But Reid refused to go. Arthur believed that neither Glass nor Reid reached his potential.

Working his contacts, Arthur arranged for Carrington, the 1973 ATA men's champion, to spend three months on the European pro tour. But Carrington, who lived his formative years on the urban streets of Elizabeth, New Jersey, stayed only two weeks. "I just didn't like being away from black people," Carrington said. "It got lonely."

When Whirlwind died, Juan Farrow was the No. 1 player in the USTA's 12-and-under division. Whirlwind believed Farrow, who lived next door, was a much stronger player than Arthur was at the same age. He told everyone, including Arthur, that Farrow was on course to greatness. Arthur supported Farrow financially throughout his junior years, but ended his support after Farrow attended Southern Illinois. Farrow won three NCAA Division II singles titles at Southern Illinois, but struggled in his early years on the pro tour.

"I just feel that Arthur feels that I'm not the kind of guy that he would like to see up there," said Farrow, interviewed in 1982 when he was 24. "I'm not the one to do the smiling, the patting on the back and going about saying things the way he would. I think that could be the reason why he's not helping me. He probably thinks I get high all the time and I'm running around after every tournament thinking this is a joyride. Maybe not. I don't know."

Carrington's coach, Sydney Llewelyn, who guided Gibson to several major championships in the late '50s, accused Arthur of "keeping doors closed to blacks," rather than opening them. "He only gave a handout here or there; Ashe never sincerely helped any of those kids," Llewelyn said. "A white man asked Ashe what he thought of Carrington and he said, 'Carrington is ghetto in dress and talk.' Ashe wiped Carrington out with one sentence."

Reid agreed. "You can't get anywhere with the big corporations unless Arthur OKs you," he once said. "I had a good chance of being sponsored by Marlboro. But they checked with Arthur and I never heard from them again. I'm sure he killed the deal."

The gist of the criticism of Arthur then was that at some point during his rise to fame he had lost his sense of identity and had sacrificed his blackness to become a hero to white America.

At a time when the nation's blacks were in a clenched-fist frame-of-mind and Muhammad Ali epitomized black authenticity, Arthur, in comparison, was viewed as an Uncle Tom. "He's not trying to identify with blacks; he's not showing any courage," Carrington once said. "I know he's not Muhammad Ali, but he could be standing taller."

In a 1975 interview, Arthur seemed to understand precisely why those who hoped to follow his path were having trouble staying on track. "In order to reach the top, you've got to begin playing tennis during the formative years and single-mindedly pursue tennis," he said. "No basketball, football or any other sport. You've got to almost divorce yourself from the black community for awhile . . . black athletes don't seem to want to do that."

Like the other black sports trailblazers of his era, Arthur could not escape the duality of his role. He learned early in his career that being the lone black tennis champion automatically made him a hero to blacks simply because he excelled in a sport dominated by whites. "The two things went hand-in-hand," Arthur once said. "The whole direction was geared by the racial prejudice because there just was no place for black kids to go."

On the day he beat Jimmy Connors in the 1975 Wimbledon final, black players at the American Tennis Association Championships in New Haven, Connecticut, halted play and danced on the courts, celebrating Arthur's stunning upset. On the final point of that victory, Arthur gave a clinched-fist salute, a gesture that, at the time, symbolized militancy/black power. Arthur quickly dispelled any notion that he was being militant, saying the salute was made in recognition of his agent and friend, Donald Dell, who years earlier had replaced Whirlwind as the most influential person in Arthur's life.

Whirlwind's son, Bobby Jr., who said his father became disappointed in Arthur when Dell became his agent, offered the most stinging assessment of Arthur's status among blacks in tennis. Bobby Jr. also believed that Arthur never gave his father the proper credit for the role he played in Arthur's success.

"I roasted (Ashe) in *Black Sports*, and I've been on Donald Dell's shit list ever since," Bobby Jr. said in a 1982 interview. "(Ashe) has been sort of distant ever since. That's his problem, not mine. If he's trying to mask his origin, that's his problem."

Dell says Bobby Jr. has shown hostility through the years, even when he does him a favor. "I got him tickets to a D.C. tournament one year, but when I bumped into him at the event he was very rough, very mad," Dell said. "He said 'I don't know why you guys didn't think more of my father and never gave me a chance.' I said 'Bobby, what the hell is your problem?' He was always pissed off and he wanted you to know he was pissed off.

"Dr. Johnson was always friendly to me and I always made a big deal of him because of Arthur. He did a hell of a lot for black tennis players. If you didn't have Dr. J, you wouldn't have had Althea and probably would never have had Arthur."

More than a year after Whirlwind's death, Arthur wrote a tribute to Whirlwind in the September 1972 issue of *Reader's Digest*. He called Whirlwind his "Most Unforgettable Character," and the story seemed Arthur's way of conceding that his decision not to attend Whirlwind's funeral might have been a serious, but honest mistake in judgment. Even that gesture did nothing for Bobby Jr.

"Bobby developed some sort of hostile attitude toward Arthur Ashe after Whirlwind died," Dr. Hubert Eaton said. "He wrote me a letter one time and said he was going to send a copy of it to the USTA magazine. Then he said, 'After I wrote it, I decided I wouldn't send it, but I wanted you to know what my thoughts were.' Bobby never thought that he got any credit for the things he did for the junior development program."

Arthur often wondered why Bobby Jr. despised him so. My take, which I relayed to Arthur more than once, was quite simple: During his formative years, Bobby Jr. probably believed that his father was more attentive to and loved Arthur more than he loved his only son.

Arthur broke a long silence and responded strongly to Bobby Jr. and other critics in an August 1975 issue of the now-defunct *Black Sports* magazine. "I do feel a tremendous sense of peer pressure and racial ethnic pressure to contribute and I do," he said. "It's not so much a debt I owe. That's something I don't adhere to anymore. I don't like being made to feel guilty. I do contribute, but no one is going to tell me how to do it or when to do it."

Arthur first learned of his protégés' accusations after reading the first draft of this book more than 20 years ago. At the time, he said nothing for a while, but the sadness in his eyes revealed the depth of his despair. He lowered his head, seemingly in meditation.

During his moment of silence, I visualized a laundry list of things Arthur had done for blacks in tennis since he had received the torch from Whirlwind. He had provided financial assistance to nearly every black junior who showed promise in the 1970s; raised millions of dollars for the United Negro College Fund by lending his name and support to a celebrity tennis exhibition each year in New York's Felt Forum; raised funds for the ATA and made personal appearances throughout the U.S. to support black causes of nearly every kind; and helped organized the National Junior Tennis League, which has introduced more than one million urban black youngsters to tennis since it was founded in 1969 by Arthur, Gene Scott, Charlie Pasarell and Sheridan Snyder.

Finally, he lifted his head and said quietly, "You know, no matter how much you do, it's never enough."

In a phone conversation weeks after learning of the bitterness that some of the young black players felt toward him, Arthur said, "That kind of stuff, you don't want revealed during your lifetime. You prefer to have those things revealed after you're gone."

The players' negative comments, however, didn't curtail Arthur's desire to bring more talented blacks into the game. He kept giving, kept searching and kept trying to guide young black pros to the highest level, despite looming changes in his lifestyle and health. Just as Whirlwind had done.

The man who affectionately became known throughout the black tennis community as Whirlwind played a key role in changing the face of tennis in America. I thank him, Althea thanked him, Arthur thanked him and a generation of black juniors thanks him for his perseverance and commitment.

His goal was to get the white establishment to open its doors, if not its heart, to black players. That's what he did, and that's why he deserves a pat on the back, not just from black America, but from all Americans.

EPILOGUE

Arthur Ashe and Althea Gibson long will be remembered for becoming the first African Americans to win major tennis championships and for touching our lives as only great champions can. Whirlwind should be remembered and recognized for providing the vision, determination and support needed for them to realize their goals.

Bonus Chapter

The author's reflections on a friend who became a sports legend

O UR FRIENDSHIP BEGAN a few years before we became teammates on Whirlwind's junior squad in 1960.

I was a 15-year-old tennis novice and Arthur Ashe was a 14-year-old prodigy on the rise when I first saw him play. He'd come to Hampton, Va. that summer to play practice sets against 18-year-old Billy Neilson, my high school's No. 1 player. Most of the time, Billy, who was bigger, stronger and smoother than Arthur, easily outclassed the rail-thin Richmond, Va. native. Still, I was mesmerized by Arthur's classic style of play, discipline and calm demeanor. Each of his strokes was laced with unexpected pace and a promise of greater power in the years to come. He moved about the court with a doesn't-matter-if-I-lose-now confidence—something Whirlwind planted within his soul years earlier—and showed the determination and potential that would carry him to greatness.

I knew then that that little guy was going to be trouble if I ever had to face him. Months later, after winning the 1958 Negro State singles title, Billy seconded my thought with this good news/bad news prediction: "I know you're good enough to be No. 1 next year, but you can forget about winning a state title. Little Ashe is starting high school next year, and he's gonna kick your ass."

And so he did, five times, in fact, including in the 1960 Virginia Interscholastic Association (VIA) championships, the black state final.

WHIRLWIND

I cherish the memories of those high school matches with Arthur, as well as the times we spent building a lifelong friendship off the court.

When I played basketball for Phenix High against Maggie Walker in Richmond, Arthur watched from the stands. Years later, William Redd, Arthur's varsity tennis teammate, told me that Arthur once pointed me out to him during a game and said, "That guy's a pretty good tennis player." Arthur frequently popped up in Hampton during the summers of the late '50s, at times driving a car.

He once spotted my date and me at a bus stop, picked us up and drove to the movie theater at breakneck speed, smiling slyly all the way. He said he wanted to make sure we got to the theater before the movie started; I said he was trying to impress my date. He showed up at a house party once. He didn't dance, except around the food table. "After watching him eat, my mama said she'd rather clothe that boy than feed him," said Bobby Miller, a classmate who hosted the party.

We occasionally exchanged letters during our college years (I was at Hampton; he at UCLA) and as young adults. At a U.S. vs. British West Indies Davis Cup tie in Richmond, Va. in 1966, he greeted my bride of a year with a kiss and chided her for not waiting to marry him. I took it as a joke at the time but later wondered if a little of Whirlwind had rubbed off on my famous friend.

Several months after he won the inaugural U.S. Open singles title in 1968, he came to Vietnam with the U.S. Davis Cup team while I was stationed there. I watched him sign autographs as he mingled comfortably with the troops. Afterward, we chatted. He wanted to know if there was anything I needed him to do. Upon his return home, he didn't forget to tell my wife he had seen me and that I was OK.

A few weeks later, I informed him in a letter that I had been wounded in action. He responded with a letter soon afterward, expressed his concern and told me that his younger brother, Johnnie, then a marine warrant officer, had been wounded in action twice during two tours in Vietnam.

He came to dinner once when I lived in Huntington, N.Y. in the '70s and spoke glowingly of an NBC photographer he had hoped to bring with him. Jeanne Moutoussamy had to work that day, but we met several months later at their wedding reception.

BONUS CHAPTER

Like so many others—I shuddered each time Arthur was beset by the health problems that eventually caused him to hang up his rackets. He was 36 when he suffered his first heart attack. He underwent a quadruple bypass operation in 1979 and tried to return to the pro tour a few months later. But a second heart attack convinced him to move on. He stayed close to the game through his roles as a Whirlwind-like benefactor to promising juniors, U.S. Davis Cup captain (1981-85), *Washington Post* tennis columnist, and *ABC, PBS,* and *HBO* tennis commentator. After I became *USA Today's* tennis writer in 1986, we spent more time together talking about, among other things, the continuing absence of blacks in pro tennis.

For many years, I was privy to his leanings and decision-making process on various issues, including what-to-do about the black juniors he inherited from Whirlwind's junior development program. We frequently discussed the changing political and social postures our nation had taken since our childhood days growing up in the segregated South. And debated the role he played/didn't play in helping various promising young black juniors.

Throughout the '70s and until his death, Arthur was tennis's most important black personality. The black tennis community looked to him first for guidance on how to increase the number of blacks on the pro circuits and address other racially sensitive matters. The white tennis establishment sought his counsel on the game's pressing issues, including multicultural concerns.

In my mind, he had become Whirlwind's successor as the Godfather of Black Tennis. I suppose that's why my 1992 trip to New York to confront him about rumors that he had contracted the deadly AIDS virus was the most difficult assignment I ever had as a journalist. Yet I knew it was one I couldn't back away from.

Throughout a lifetime steeped in daunting challenges, Arthur's ability to make light of taut moments was one of his most endearing traits. So I really shouldn't have been surprised that spring morning when, just hours before he announced to the world that he had been diagnosed with AIDS, Arthur sprayed a smile on my troubled face. After opening the door of his Eastside apartment in New York with weary eyes and that distinctive nasal voice, Arthur chuckled, "I hope you got some sleep last night because I sure didn't." I needed something to ease my anxiety of the past 24 hours and he knew it.

On April 5, 1992, I made a business trip to New York to ask my friend—on the record—if he was dying of AIDS. He had assumed I was there to discuss my role in updating his book—*Hard Road to Glory*—his three-volume history of the Black Athlete in America. Published in 1987, Arthur had asked me to pour through the hundreds of letters he'd received requesting corrections and scores of sports articles he'd saved on the exploits of teen phenoms Tiger Woods, Venus and Serena Williams and other young black achievers in sports.

At some point, I abruptly changed the subject and told him that I had come specifically to ask him if he had AIDS. Since I didn't preface the question with our mutually agreed upon coded phrase, 'Just between me and you,' he knew the question was posed by Doug Smith, *USA Today* journalist, not Doug Smith, the friend. A long pause preceded Arthur's answer, which came in the form of a request. "Give my phone number to your editor and have him call me around 4 p.m." He then asked me to call him that night after he had spoken with my editor.

Now convinced that the rumors were true, I left Arthur's apartment that afternoon wondering how to ease the pain that ricocheted through my body before settling deep in my heart. Through teary eyes and on wobbly feet, I followed the sounds of my footsteps to New York's St. Patrick's Cathedral where I knelt in agony for a long while and prayed for a miracle. 'Please Lord, don't let my friend die. Not now, he's still so young.'

Back in my room at the Elysee Hotel, I wiped away tears, regained my professional footing and called Gene Policinski, *USA Today's* managing editor of sports.

"Well, is it true?" Policinski asked.

"Looks that way," I said, "but he wants you to call him at home. Maybe he wants to try to talk you out of running with it."

Before asking for details, Policinski directed me to call tennis editor Steve Ballard. I told Steve that while I was pretty sure the rumors were true, Arthur never admitted that he had AIDS.

In his phone conversation with Policinski, Arthur again refused to confirm suspicions. Later, in a telephone conference call with my editors and me, *USA Today's* editor Peter Prichard directed us to confirm the story before our 11 p.m. deadline. No one did and in our phone conversation that night, Arthur breathed a sigh of relief when I told him that *USA Today's* policy precluded the paper from publishing a story based on unnamed sources and that I doubted if we would break the story without him—or someone else—confirming it on the record.

"Well, I hope you're right," he said. "I'll check the wires tonight and the papers first thing in the morning. Come by in the morning and we'll talk then."

Like Arthur, I was relieved that nothing about his illness or my visit to his home was mentioned in *USA Today* or any other newspaper. He believed that his illness was a personal matter, something that he shouldn't have to share with the public. He loathed being forced to disclose his illness and believed that once he did, he would be ostracized, treated like someone with leprosy.

When I arrived at his home the following morning, Arthur and I joined *Sports Illustrated's* Frank Deford in the study. Arthur said then that he would disclose his illness. Deford, who had collaborated with Arthur on *Portrait in Motion,* a year in Arthur's life, helped structure Arthur's AIDS announcement, which Arthur delivered later that day. Arthur gave me the first on-the-record interview on his illness. Before I had a chance to query him on his illness, in a voice simmering with rage, he peppered me with questions regarding the source of the story. At times, I buckled.

"Who made the call?" he asked.
"Can't tell you," I said.
"Who made the call," he asked again.
"Arthur, I can't tell you."
"Did Bobby Johnson make the call?"
"Can't tell you."
"Did Bobby Johnson make the call?"
"No," I said.
"Who took the call?"
"Can't tell you."
"Who took the call?"
"Arthur, I can't tell you."

"Did you take the call?"
"No," I lied.
"Why did you come here?"
"Because it's my job, Arthur, and I wasn't going to allow anyone else to come here and do my job."

Calmness settled over him after our last exchange, and just like that, the fury that I had never seen in him before seeped away.

Two points on my exchange with Arthur:

- I wasn't surprised that Arthur thought Whirlwind's son, Bobby Jr., might have been the caller. Bobby Jr. often struck out at Arthur in his later years. Friends in the media had told Arthur that Bobby Jr. periodically made disparaging remarks about him.
- I've never revealed the name of the caller to anyone, including *USA Today* editors and I never will. But, for some reason, I had this annoying feeling in my soul that had I told Arthur that I had received the call, considering the circumstances, I might have succumbed to the urgency in his voice and broken a confidence. I suspect that's why I lied.

In his first interview on his illness, Arthur said doctors believed he contracted HIV, the virus that causes AIDS, during one of two blood transfusions (December 1979 and June 1983) when he underwent heart bypass operations. He tested positive for AIDS after brain surgery in September 1988. He said he had planned to reveal his illness later, when he felt close to death. "Actually, in a way I'm relieved that it's finally going to be in the open," he said. "I was never concerned about myself. I was concerned about how Jeanne (wife) and Camera (daughter) would feel if people treated me differently."

When I interviewed Jeanne later that morning, she, too, seemed as if a boulder had been lifted from their shoulders. "In some respect, I am relieved," Jeanne said. "It's like coming out of a closet. I cannot tell you how many times friends, who did not know, would say something in reference to AIDS. You feel like you're hiding something. But I'm angered, too, because I believe that Arthur deserves to be treated better."

Many, including media columnists, expressed similar feelings to me and to others at *USA Today*. Some left damning voice mail messages or venomous letters, like this one:

> *Dear Mr. Smith,*
> *I have learned today of the despicable part you played in the 'outing' of Arthur Ashe. You must be really proud of your betrayal of someone that you knew from childhood and with whom you served in the Army, and someone who probably trusted you. Why he or anybody else ever puts trust in a lowlife dirt bag like you, I don't know. I hope that you and the scumbags that sent you on your sleezy (sic) little mission suffer a worse fate than Mr. Ashe. You are a piece of shit and so are the vermin you work for.' Signed K.O. B.*

My worst moment, however, came as I paused from writing a story in my hotel room that afternoon and watched Arthur break down emotionally as he read his AIDS press release. In one day, I saw a good friend show a range of emotion—from rage to extreme sadness—I never dreamed he possessed. Watching Arthur break down during that televised announcement haunted me for several months. My discomfort grew more intense when many of Arthur's supporters and admirers, including several of my colleagues in the media, condemned me for forcing a friend to take a course of action that he clearly did not want to take. I felt conflicted—indeed responsible—for putting him through a heart-wrenching ordeal. Emotionally, I'd never felt lower. But in time, I was able to smile again, mainly because of what Arthur did with the remaining 10 months of his life. These actions lifted him from superstar level to American hero:

- Less than four months after making the announcement, Arthur assumed a productive leadership role in the AIDS fight. He formed the Arthur Ashe Foundation for the Defeat of AIDS and raised millions of dollars to combat this disease, which continues to alarm the world community and has devastated several African countries.
- He became an AIDS activist and helped ease the anxiety that many people had about interacting with friends and loved ones

who had contracted the disease. In a tribute, Sen. Ted Kennedy (D-Mass.) said Arthur "brought dignity and hope to people living with HIV, consistently speaking out for desperately needed health care and support services and against senseless discrimination." In December 1992, Arthur received the first AIDS Leadership Award from the Harvard AIDS Institute.
- He wrote a best-selling book, *Days of Grace* (with Arnold Rampersad, published in 1993 by Alfred A. Knopf, Inc., New York), an inspiring account of his struggle to survive what he knew would be a losing battle.

A day after I confronted him on the AIDS issue at his New York home, Arthur said that his plan had been to keep his illness secret until he was close to death. Had he followed that plan I doubt if he would now be remembered as a sports legend and that the U.S. Open's stadium court would bear his name.

In a *USA Today* commentary two months before Arthur died, I indicated that I wished I could say that I did what I did because I knew it would force Arthur to do what he had to do. Bottom line is I went to confront Arthur at his home that day; feeling inside it was something I had to do. I'm no longer troubled by that decision. I'm at peace about it mainly because of what Arthur achieved in the aftermath.

At times, I considered blaming Whirlwind for causing me to endure such agony. After all, had it not been for the good doctor, Arthur never would have become a superstar and I, therefore, wouldn't have knocked on his door that fateful day. On the other hand, if Arthur hadn't followed the gonna-be-a-tennis-star script, which pretty much was designed and directed by Whirlwind, I wouldn't have had a tale to tell.

Appendix A
Highest Ranked African-American Pro

Michael Baz

Arthur Ashe—No. 2
Birthdate: July 10, 1943
Place of Birth: Richmond, Virginia
Deceased: February 6, 1993

ATP Tour History
Career singles titles: 33
Singles finalist: 32
Career doubles titles: 18
Doubles finalist: 28

Best Results at Grand Slams
Australian Open—champion (1970), finalist (1971), career record—16-3
French Open—quarterfinalist (1971), career record—25-8
Wimbledon—champion (1975), career record—27-8
U.S. Open—champion (1968), career record—38-9

APPENDIX A

African-American male pros on ATP circuit since the Open Era (1968–2003)

Name	Highest Ranking	Year
Arthur Ashe	2	1976
MaliVai Washington	11	1992
Chip Hooper	17	1982
James Blake	28	2002
Marcel Freeman	46	1986
Bryan Shelton	55	1992
Rodney Harmon	56	1983
Todd Nelson	58	1986
Steve Campbell	78	1998
Bruce Foxworth	146	1979
Martin Blackman	158	1994
Juan Farrow	227	1985
Mashiska Washington	290	1999

Source: ATP

Appendix B
First African American in Grand Slam events

Althea Gibson
Date of Birth: Aug. 25, 1927
Place of Birth: Silver, South Carolina
Died: September 28, 2003

Tennis Career History

The dominant player of the late 1950s, Gibson was the first African American allowed to play in the U.S. National Championships (now U.S. Open). Gibson won 56 singles and doubles titles during her amateur career. Her major titles include:

French singles champion—1956
Italian singles champion—1956
Wimbledon singles champion—1957–58
U.S. National singles champion—1957–58
Australian doubles champion (w/Shirley Fry)—1957
French doubles champion (w/Angela Buxton)—1956
Wimbledon doubles champion (w/Buxton)—1956
Wimbledon doubles champion (w/Darlene Hard)—1957
Wimbledon doubles champion (w/Maria Bueno)—1958

Golf Career

Gibson, the first African American on the LPGA tour, played in 171 tournaments (1963–77) without a title.

APPENDIX B

African-American female pros on WTA Tour in the Open Era (1968–2003)

Name	Highest ranking	Year
Venus Williams	1	2000–01
Serena Williams	1	2002
Zina Garrison	4	1990
Chanda Rubin	6	1996
Lori McNeil	9	1988
Leslie Allen	17	1981
Camille Benjamin	27	1984
Kim Sands	44	1984
Diane Morrison	50	1979
Stacey Martin	58	1989
Renee Blount	63	1981
Katrina Adams	67	1989
Micheala Washington	81	1984
Mashona Washington	103	2002
Andrea Buchanan	106	1981
Shenay Perry	143	2003
Angela Haynes	194	2003

Index

Adams, Katrina, 160, 164, 182
AIDS, 173–174, 176–177
Alabama, University of, 84
Alfred A. Knopf, Inc., 178
Algonquin Club, 87
Ali, Muhammad, 166
All England Croquet and Lawn Tennis Club, 42
Allar, Marcia, 151
Allen, Leslie, 62, 113, 160–161, 164, 182
American Lawn Tennis, 59
American Professional Football Association, 28
American Tennis Association (ATA), xiv, 4–5, 41, 48
   founding of, 43–44
   Junior Development Committee, 5
   National Championships, xiv, 44–46, 54–55, 72–73, 79, 108, 166
   National Intercollegiate Championships, 80
   National Interscholastic Championship, 72, 79, 103, 109
   National Junior Championship, 80, 85
   USLTA and, 45, 47, 58, 95
Anne Spencer House, 156
Arizona, University of, 106
Arthur Ashe Foundation for the Defeat of AIDS, 177
Ashe, Arthur
   as AIDS activist, 177–178
   American Tennis Association (ATA) tournaments and, 76, 99–100, 102, 106–107
   attending UCLA, 106–108, 112, 118, 124, 136, 172
   coached by Dr. Robert Walter Johnson, 80, 87–88, 95, 98–104, 107–108, 124, 136, 171, 178
   coached by Ronald Charity, 73–74
   daughter, Camera, and, 176
   Davis Cup and, 108, 119, 172–173
   friendship with Donald Dell, 71, 152, 166
   Hall of Fame and, xv
   Hard Road to Glory and, 174
   health problems of, 173–176
   influence on future generations, 163–166, 168, 173
   jobs after playing career, 173
   legend of, 113, 162, 169, 179–180
   living in St. Louis, 103–106
   meeting Dr. Robert Walter Johnson, 72–73
   missing the funeral of Dr. Robert Walter Johnson, 151–152, 167
   Negro National Interscholastic Championships and, xii, 100
   playing with Bobby Davis, 87–88, 99
   playing with Dennis Ralston, 152
   playing Marty Riessen, 141, 152
   playing with Dr. Robert Walter Johnson, 106–107
   playing with Ronald Charity, 106–107
   playing with Willis Fennell, 80
   playing with Willis Thomas, 81, 87, 89
   racism and, 102–103, 105, 118, 163–164
   respect for Althea Gibson, 62
   response to criticism, 167–168
   U.S. Clay Court Championship and, 118
   U.S. Hard Court Championship and, 118
   U.S. Intercollegiate Championship and, 118
   U.S. National Championships/U.S. Open and, 95–96, 119, 124, 155, 172, 178–179
   USLTA Interscholastic Championships and, xiv, 98, 100–101, 105

INDEX

Virginia Negro State High School Championships and, xii, 100, 171
  wife, Jeanne Moutousammy, and, 172, 176
  Wimbledon and, 107, 152–153, 166, 179
Ashe, Arthur Sr., 73–74, 103
Ashe, Johnnie, 73, 172
Ashmun Institute, *see* Lincoln University
Atlanta University, 30
Australian Open, 179

Baker, Bertram, 48, 60, 92–96, 98, 106, 115
Ballard, Lula, 45
Ballard, Steve, 174
Benjamin, Camille, 182
Black Hand Club, 22
Black Panther Party, 117
Black Sports, 166
Blackman, Clifford, 45
Blackman, Martin, 180
Blake, James, 162, 180
Blake, Thomas, 162
Blount, Renee, 182
Blue Vein Society, The, 53
Bollettieri, Nick, xv, 138, 160
Bonds, Alex, 17
Boulware, Ralph, 38–39
Braddock, Jim, 41
Branson, Herman, 148
Braswell, Leon, 38
Brooke Field Park, 73
Brooklyn Dodgers, 2, 83
Brooks, James, 151
Brotherhood of Sleeping Car Porters, 28
Brough, A. Louise, 60
Brown, Bob, 49
Brown, Charles, 85, 87–88
Brown, Edgar G., 45
Brown, James, 117
Bryant, James Jr., xii–xiii
Bryant, James Sr., xii
Buchanan, Andrea, 182
Buchholz, Cliff, 104–105
Buchholz, Earl "Butch" Jr., 104–105
Budge, J. Donald, 46, 48
Bunche, Ralph, 2, 60

Busick, Jim, 102
Buxton, Angela, 62

Campbell, Steve, 180
Calhoun, Thomas, 127
Calloway, Cab, 53
Cannon, George D., 21, 23–24, 53, 148
Canton Bulldogs, 28
Carrington, Arthur, 118, 160, 164–165
Carter Baron Tennis Courts, 107
Carter, L.L. "Battleship," 19
Central High School (Little Rock, Ark.), 84
Central Intercollegiate Athletic Association (CIAA) (also Colored Intercollegiate Athletic Association), 1, 19, 22, 28, 52
Central State University, 45, 54–56, 72
Channels, Isadore, 44–45
Charity, Ronald, 73–74, 106–107
Chautauqua Tennis Club, 43
Chicago, University of, 24
Chippey, Arthur, 5
Civil Rights Bill of 1875, 12
Clifton Park, 101
Clover, William L., 4
Cohen, Richard, 46
Cole, Nat King, 53
Coleman, Beverly, 80, 109–110, 160
Coleman, Walter, 159
Columbia University, 22
Community Funeral Home, 76
Connors, Jimmy, 166
Convivial Coterie, 53
Cook, Ralph, 43
Cook, William Lionel, 5, 39–40
Cookson, Bob, 163–164
Cosmopolitan Tennis Club, 46, 55, 59
Costen, Wayman, 148
Court Street Baptist Church, 150–151
Creasy, Hortense, 136, 141–142, 145
Creasy-Rosser, Erdice, 68, 86, 124, 129, 147–149, 154–155
Cunningham, Horace "Red," 85–86, 95, 99–100

Darden, Colgate, 4, 144
Dartmouth University, 22

INDEX

Davis, Billy, xiv
Davis, Bobby, 85, 87–88, 99, 160
Davis, Nana, 57
Davis, Wilbert, 94–95, 102
Deford, Frank, 175
Dell, Donald, 70–71, 152, 166–167
Devine, Rock, 135
Diamond Hill Baptist Church, 148, 150–151
Dickey, John Miller, 23
Dinkins, David, 57–58, 62
Dixie Play Girls, 49
Dot Records, 61
Dreamland Auditorium, 34, 49
Druid Hill Park, 44
DuBois, W.E.B., 52
Duke University, 147
Dunbar High School (Lynchburg, Va.), 3, 76, 85, 127

Easterling, Carl, 112
Eastern Grass Court Championships, 60
Eaton, Hubert Jr., 132
Eaton, Hubert Sr., 5, 38–40, 50, 54–57, 63, 65, 78, 95–96, 112, 115–116, 132, 147, 151, 167
Eckford, Elizabeth, 84
Eckstine, Billie, 53
Edmonds, Helen, 66–67, 135
Elizabeth City College, *see* Elizabeth City State University
Elizabeth City State Normal School, *see* Elizabeth City State University
Elizabeth City State University, 11, 124, 133
Emerson, Roy, 108
English, Hallie "Peggy," *see* Johnson, Hallie "Peggy" English
Erie Tennis Club, 127
Evert, Chris, xv

F.W. Woolworth, 104
Farrow, Juan
  coached by Dr. Robert Walter Johnson, 137–143, 148–149, 151
  comparisons to Arthur Ashe, 140, 165
  development into a junior champion, 142–143, 153
  playing with Bobby Johnson III, 140–141
  playing with Chip Hooper, 141, 143
  playing professionally, 165, 180
  relationship with Arthur Ashe, 140, 164–165
Farrow, Paul, 139
Felt Forum, 168
Fennell, Willis, 77, 79–81
Ferguson, Andrew, xiv
Ferrin, James, 70
Finney, William, 24
Fisk University, 104
FitzGibbon, Herb, 101
Florida A&M University, 57
Ford Foundation, 135
Ford, Herman, 151
Foxworth, Bruce, 180
Freeman, Clyde, 65, 95, 132
Freeman, Harold, 65, 95, 132
Freeman, Henry, 43
Freeman, Lucille, 65, 116, 132
Freeman, Marcel, 164, 180
French Championships, 60, 179
Froehling, Frank, 105
Fugate, Marcus, 162
Furlonge, C.W., 39, 71

Gant, Rufus, xi–xii, 83
Garrison, Zina, 45, 62, 160, 162–164, 182
Geneva Medical School, University of, 130, 135
George P. Phenix High School (Hampton, Va.), xi–xii, 79, 85, 172
Gibson, Althea
  ATA National Championships and, 45, 54–57, 73
  coached by Dr. Robert Walter Johnson, xv, 54–58, 63, 122, 151
  coached by Sydney Llewelyn, 60, 165
  education of, 57
  growing up, 56–57, 111
  letter from Alice Marble to USLTA, 2, 59
  life after tennis, 61–62, 164
  as pioneer, 58–62, 108–109, 113, 122, 162, 169, 181

INDEX

playing style of, 61
United States Lawn Tennis Association (USLTA) and, 2
U.S. National Championships and, 2, 58, 60, 95
Wimbledon and, 60, 63–64, 110
winning the French Championships, 60
Gittens, Frances, 59
Glass, Luis, 108–110, 135, 164–165
Glass, Sydney, 109–110, 135
Gonzales, Pancho, 79
Grand Central Station, 27, 29, 121
Gray, Fran, 62
Greene, W. Henry "Stud", 50–51, 54, 130
Gregg, Arthur, 38
Grim, Harold, 24
Guernsy, Frank, 65

Hall, Grant P., 20
Hamlet, George, 159
Hampton Institute (Hampton University), xii, xiv, 1, 19, 21, 25, 44, 87, 104, 106, 116, 133, 164–165, 172
Happy Land Lake Club, 64, 68
Hardwick, Mary, 59
Hare, Charles E., 46
Harlem Globetrotters, 40, 61
Harlem Rens, 44
Harmon, Rodney, 160, 162–163, 180
Harris, Tom, 5
Hart, Doris, 60
Harum, Al, 3
Harvard University, 22, 24
Harvard AIDS Institute, 178
Hawes, Thomas, xiii-xiv
Haynes, Angela, 182
Heidelberg, University of, 135
Henry, Crawford, 79
Heron, H.W., 44
Hill City Recreation Club, 48
Hill High School (Potsdam, N.Y.), 70
Hill, Richard, 24
Hillside High School (Durham, N.C.), 79
Hilton, Gracie, 159
Hitler, Adolph, 40
Hoage, D. Ivison, 44, 48

Holiday, Billie, 53
Holmes, Tally, 43–45
Hooper, Chip, 141, 164, 180
Hooper, Lawrence, 141
Horne, Lena, 53
Howard University, 1, 19, 22, 25, 28, 50, 134
Howard University School of Medicine, 130
Howard, James T., 44
Hubbard, Fletcher, 151
Hudlin, Richard, 104
Hurt, Eddie, 28–29
Hutcherson, Carl, 147
Hutcherson, Sam, 65

Icely, L.B., 46
International Tennis Hall of Fame, xv, 45
Irwin, Nina, 55

Jack and Jill, 67
Jackson, Nat, 49, 56
James, Arthur, 24
Jenkins, Wilbur, 127
John L. Roper Lumber Company, 8–9
Johnson, Annie Pate (first wife), 14–18, 22, 27–28, 30–35, 66, 126, 129
Johnson, Bobby III (grandson), 131, 140–142, 155
Johnson, Eileen Eldorado "Dr. El" (sister), 26–27, 130–131, 133–137, 147–149, 153, 155
Johnson, Elaine (sister), 26–27, 76
Johnson, Eva (sister), 9, 11–12, 15, 26, 32–33, 76, 133–134, 144–145, 154
Johnson, Fred, 55
Johnson, Hallie "Peggy" English (second wife), 30, 32–35, 48, 64, 66–68, 121, 126–127, 154
Johnson, Hiawatha, 151
Johnson, Jerry John "Papa Jerry" (father), 6–13, 15–17, 26, 31, 33–35, 38, 40, 50, 64, 129, 133, 144–145, 152, 155
Johnson, Julian (grandson), 131
Johnson, Lance (grandson), 131
Johnson, Lyndon B., 117

186

INDEX

Johnson, "Mama Nancy" Scott
  (mother), 7–9, 11–12, 15–17, 26, 34–35,
  36–37, 76, 121, 133–134, 144, 152
Johnson, Nerissa Lange, 74, 123, 129–132
Johnson, Robert "Bobby" Jr. (son),
  birth of, 29–30
  coaching players, 74, 79, 81, 86–87, 167
  conflict with Arthur Ashe, 74, 98, 125,
    151–152, 166–167, 175–176
  education of, 123, 127, 129–132
  playing tennis, 73, 122, 126–128
  playing U.S. Nationals, 129
  raised by and/or relationship with his
    father, 34, 50, 119, 126–133, 140–142,
    148, 155
  service in U.S. Army, 129
  talking about his father, 104, 109–110,
    112, 126–129, 132, 146
  wife and, 74, 123, 129–132
Johnson, Robert Walter "Whirlwind",
  ailing, 146–148
  American Tennis Association (ATA)
    and, 4–5, 48, 81, 92–98, 109, 112–116,
    132
  birth of, 9
  burial of, 156–157
  Central Intercollegiate Athletic
    Association (CIAA) and, 1, 50
  children fathered by, 11, 29, 67, 119,
    152–153
  coaching other sports, 28–30, 36
  commissioner of tennis for Virginia
    Negro high schools, 3
  death of, 148–150
  disciples of, 160–161
  Dreamland Auditorium and, 49
  education of, 11, 13–14, 16–19, 22, 25–26,
    31, 34, 126
  friendship and partnership with Dr.
    Hubert Eaton Sr., 5, 38–40, 54–56,
    65, 71, 96, 115, 147
  funeral of, 145, 150–152, 156
  growing up in Plymouth, N.C., 9–11,
    150, 152
  honored by Lincoln University, 148
  hunting and, 49–50
  International Tennis Hall of Fame
    and, xv
  jobs held by, 10–11, 26–27, 121
  junior development program and, xi–xv,
    5, 71–74, 76, 78–80, 83–96, 108–114,
    117–119, 121, 129–130, 135–139, 144, 161
  letter to William F. Riordau, 89–91
  marriages of, see Johnson, Annie Pate;
    Johnson, Hattie "Peggy" English
  medical internship of, 34
  medical practice of, 36–39, 64, 132
  mental rest club and, 51–52
  mentor to Althea Gibson, xv, 55–57, 63,
    122, 136, 161, 169
  mentor to Arthur Ashe, xv, 73–74,
    76–77, 80, 82, 87–88, 95–96, 98–104,
    107–108, 111, 119, 136, 156, 161, 169,
    171, 178
  Negro National Interscholastic
    Championship and, 4–5
  origin of nickname "Whirlwind," 21
  parties thrown by, 65–66, 68
  playing football, 11, 14, 16, 19–22, 25, 28,
    41
  playing tennis, 39–42, 48, 54, 57–58, 65,
    68, 106–107, 127–128
  race relations and, 2–3, 6, 12–13, 52–54,
    68–69, 75–76, 78, 83–85, 87–89, 104,
    117–118, 135–137, 156, 168
  relationship with parents, 15, 35, 76, 145
  scouting talent, 49, 86, 137–138
  siblings of, 9–12, 26–27, 34, 40, 130,
    133–135, 137, 153
  standing in community, 64–65, 153–154
  USLTA Interscholastic Championships
    and, xiii, 1–5, 69–71, 76, 78–79, 88,
    98, 105, 109, 144, 156
  will of, 154, 159
  womanizing by, 11, 14–15, 22, 30, 51–52,
    54, 66–68, 172
Johnson, Roy (brother), 10, 12, 26, 134
Johnson, Rupert (brother), 26–27, 34, 40,
  134
Johnson, Ruth Olivia (sister), 12, 26–27
Johnson, Samuel DeLeon (brother), 12,
  26–27, 40

INDEX

Johnson, Victoria (sister), 9–12, 15–17, 26, 32, 36–37, 133, 149
Johnson Moore, Carolyn Waltee (daughter), 67–68, 119, 145, 153
   disciplined by her father, 123
   education of, 123–124
   interest in boys, 122
   playing tennis, 122
   relationship with her father, 120–125
   talking about her father, 120–125
   thoughts about Arthur Ashe, 124–125, 151–152
Johnson Reid, Nona (daughter), 152–153, 159
Jones, Clifton, 15
Jones, William "Babe", 5, 113, 122

Kennedy, Edward "Ted", 178
Kentucky Derby, 51
King, Billie Jean, 61–62
King, Elton, 5
King, Martin Luther Jr., 84, 117, 123
Knapp, Barbara, 60
Ku Klux Klan, 12, 17

Laney, Al, 46
Lange, Nerissa, see Johnson, Nerissa Lange
Langhorne, Ruth, 136
Lawson, Agnes, 49, 65
Lee, Beth, 107
Lee, Edgar, xiv, 95
Leigh University, 24
Lenoir, Bill, xiv, 100–101, 105
Leonard, Emma, 44
Lincoln University, 17–27, 34, 36, 38–39, 41, 44, 50, 52–53, 134, 146–148
Lincoln, Abraham, 23
Livas, Henry, 79–80, 83, 100
Llewelyn, Sydney, 60, 165
Logan, Bonnie, 108–109, 111–113
Logan, George, 111
Lomax, Flora, 45
London High School (Bethesda, Md.), 79
Louis, Joe, 41, 58
Lucas, John, 135

Lucy, Autherine, 84
Lynch, Hugh, 101
Lynchburg General Hospital, 76, 147, 149
Lynchburg Tennis Association, 155–156

Macci, Rick, xv
MacKay, Barry, 5
Maggie Walker High School (Richmond, Va.), xii, 100, 172
Malcolm X, 117–118
Mall Tennis Club, 58
Malloy, Richard, 79
Maloney, Pauline Wheaton, 76
Marble, Alice, 2, 59
Marlboro Award, 136
Marshall, Carter, 51
Martin, Julius "June Bug", 72
Martin, Stacey, 182
Maryland State Championships, 88, 102, 111
Massie, William, 147, 149
Mather Academy (Camden, S.C.), 123
McCard, Harry S., 43
McCauley, E.L., 5
McCrea, James, 52, 148
McDaniel, Jimmie, 46, 48
McEnroe, John, 143
McEvans, Gwen, 109–110
McGill, John, xiii–xiv
McGriff, John Jr., 5
McNeil, Lori, 62, 160, 163–164, 182
Mechanics & Farmers Bank, 94
Megginson, Roosevelt, 3, 70, 148
Meharry Medical College, 31, 33–34, 126
Merchant of Venice, 24
Michigan State University, 106
Miller, Bobby, 172
Miller, Ethel Reid, 109–110, 121
Miller, Victor, 3, 70, 148
Mitchell, Harold, 46
Morehouse College, 44
Morgan State University, 19–20, 28–29
Morgan, C.L. "Big Boy", 19
Morgan, Ephraim Franklin, 20
Morgan, J.D., 106
Morgan, Vernon, 95

INDEX

Morris Brown College, 29–30
Morrison, Diane, 182
Mortimer, Angela, 60
Moutoussamy, Jeanne, 172
Mudd, John, 107
Muhammad, Elijah, 117

NAACP (National Association for the Advancement of Colored People), 84
Nation of Islam, 117
National Junior Tennis League, 168
National League Park, 25
Navratilova, Martina, 45
Negro National Interscholastic Championships, xii, 4–5, 100
Neilly, Timothy, 162
Neilson, Dorothy, 87
Neilson, Herman "Buck", xiv, 87, 116
Neilson, William "Billy", 85–87, 99–100, 116, 171
Nelson, Todd, 164, 180
New Chapel Baptist Church, 150
New Jersey Governor's Commission on Physical Fitness, 61
New York Amsterdam News, 96
New York Herald Tribune, 46
New York Post, xiv
New York State Assembly, 94
New York University, 133
Newman, Butch, 105
Newsday, 161
Newton, Huey, 117
Nicholson, Nellie, 44
Nobel Peace Prize, 2, 60, 117
Norfolk Mission College, 9
Norgoner, Carl, 3
Norman, Gerald F., 44
North Carolina A&T College, 103
North Carolina Central College, 111, 134
North Carolina Teachers' College, 27
Notre Dame, University of, 19

Okker, Tom, 119
Olympics – 1912, 28
Olympics – 1936, 40

Omega Psi Phi fraternity, 22, 38, 147
Orange Bowl, 145, 162
Orange Lawn Tennis Association, 59
Owens, Jesse, 40

Palmer Memorial High School (Sedalia, N.C.), 123, 127
Parker, Larry, 105
Parks, Gordon Jr., 65
Parks, Rosa, 84
Pasarell, Charlie, 105, 168
Pate, Annie, see Johnson, Annie Pate
Pate, Mother, 16
Penn Relays, 52
Penzold, Edmund "Teddy", 3–4, 6, 70, 144–145
Penzold, Lucy, 4, 144
Perry, Shenay, 182
Peters, Roumania, 54–55
Phillips Exter High School (Exeter, N.H.), 70
Pigskin Club, 107
Plessy vs. Ferguson, 12
Plymouth Box and Panel Company, 10
Plymouth Elementary School, 11
Poe, Edgar Allen, 134
Poindexter, Hildrus A., 20–25, 53–54
Policinski, Gene, 174
Prairie View Hospital, 34, 39, 49
Prairie View State College, 127–129
Pressinger, Pete, 70
Price, Oracene, 164
Prichard, Peter, 175
Princeton Seminary College, see Princeton University
Princeton University, xiv, 23
Pruden, Joe, 159
Pullman Company, 27–28
Purcell, Mel, 143

Rainford, Julius, 44
Ralston, Dennis, 152
Rampersad, Arnold, 178
Randolph, Asa Philip, 28
Reader's Digest, 167
Redd, William, 172

INDEX

Reese, Eddie, 142
Reid, Horace, 117–118, 164–165
Rhetta, B.M., 43–44
Rickey, Branch, 2, 83
Riessen, Marty, 141
Riggs, Bobby, 65
Rivermont Baptist Church, 151
Roberts, Al, 79
Roberts, Leo, 51
Robinson, Bill "Bojangles", 53
Robinson, Hattie, 64
Robinson, Haywood Jr., 151
Robinson, Jackie, 2, 6, 58, 83
Robinson, Mattie, 37
Rockland State Hospital, 135
Rockne, Knute, 19
Rosewall, Ken, 61, 95
Rosser, Irving, 68
Rotunda Hospital, 135
Rubin, Chanda, 62, 164, 182
Ryland, Robert, 95

Sadri, John, 143
Saitch, Eyre, 44
Sam Houston College, 29
Sands, Kim, 182
Saperstein, Abe, 40
Scott, Gene, 168
Scott, Mary Celia (grandmother), 8
Scott, Nancy (great-grandmother), 8
Scott, Nancy "Mama Nancy" (mother), see Johnson, "Mama Nancy" Scott
Screen, Robert M., 61
Seale, Bobby, 117
Seay, C.W., 151
SFX, 71
Shaw University, 13–17, 19, 25, 39
Shelton, Bryan, 164, 180
Short Journey Elementary School, 133
Sides, Bennie, 48, 65
Simpson, Linwood, 108–109, 135
Sinatra, Frank, 151
Smith, Doug,
    American Tennis Association and, xiv
    doubles partner James Bryant Jr. and, xii-xiii

friendship with Arthur Ashe, 161, 163, 167–168, 171–178
guidance from Dr. Robert Walter Johnson, xi-xii, 159, 161, 171, 178
as journalist, xiv, 161, 163, 173–177
junior development team and, xi-xiv, 171
Negro National Interscholastic Championships and, xii
playing Arthur Ashe, xii, 100
playing basketball, 172
student at George P. Phenix High School, xi, 100, 172
student at Hampton Institute, xiv, 172
USLTA Interscholastic Championships and, xii-xiii
Virginia Negro State High School Championships and, xii, 171
Smith, Howard M., 44
Smith, James, 38
Smith, Russell, 44
Smith, Sylvester, 44, 93, 96
Snyder, Sheridan, 168
South Carolina State University, 44, 58
Southern Illinois University, 165
Southern Railway, 75
Sports Illustrated Award of Merit, 112
St. Louis Armory, 104
St. Mary's Academy (Windsor, Canada), 123
St. Patrick's Cathedral, 174
St. Paul's College, 22, 25
Stewart, George, xiv, 58, 95
Straley, Walt, 79
Stubbs, William H., 34
Sumner High School (St. Louis, Mo.), 106
Supreme Court, 12, 74–75, 84

Taylor, James C., 16, 33–34
Taylor, Rob, 12
Teltscher, Eliot, 143
Tennessee A&I, 104
Thomas, Willis, 81, 86–87, 160, 163
Thornhill, M.W., 76
Thorpe, Jim, 28
Thron, Aljoscho, 162
Tilden, William "Big Bill", 45

190

INDEX

Till, Emmett, 84
Toodle Cemetery, 156
Towe, Edison Louis Jr., 50
Trabert, Tony, 95
Trafton, Henry, 8
Trenton Nighthawks, 49
True Holiness Church, 151
Truman, Harry, 2
Tupper, Henry M., 16
Tuskegee Institute, 44, 46

U.S. National Championships (U.S. Open), 2, 58, 60, 172, 178–179
UCLA, 106–108, 112, 118, 124, 136, 164, 172
United Negro College Fund, 168
United States Lawn Tennis Association (USLTA), 2, 42, 45, 47, 92, 136
   Delaware State Championship, 87
   Interscholastic Championships, xi, 1, 5, 69–71, 76, 79, 88, 106, 148
   National Clay Court Championships, 60
   National Father/Son Clay Court Tournament, 127
   National Indoor Championships, 58
   National Junior Championships, 87
USA Today, 161, 163, 173–178
Utopian Tennis Club, 94

Van Buren, Lillian, 59
Vanderbilt University, 136
Virginia Negro State High School Championships, xii, 85, 171
Virginia Seminary College, 28–29, 36, 67
Virginia Union University, 5, 16, 19, 73
Virginia, University of, xiii, 1, 3, 69–70, 144

Walker, Carrie, 30
Walker, O.G., 30, 114, 136
Ward, Holcombe, 47
Washington Post, 5, 173

Washington Redskins, 50, 52, 155
Washington Tennis & Education Foundation, 160
Washington, MaliVai, 162, 180
Washington, Mashiska, 180
Washington, Mashona, 182
Washington, Micheala, 182
Washington, Ora, 45
Watanabe, Tina, 135
Wayne, John, 61
Weir, Reginald, 45–46, 58, 95
Wells, Jake, 58
West Side Tennis Club, 58, 60
West Virginia State University, 20, 25
Wheeler, John, 5, 94
Wilberforce University, 22
Wilkerson, John, 163–164
Wilkerson, John F.N., 43
Williams, Joe, xiii-xiv, 87–88, 95, 99–100, 113
Williams, Richard, 164
Williams, Serena, 62, 162, 164, 174, 182
Williams, Toni, 58
Williams, Venus, 62, 162, 164, 174, 182
Wills-Moody, Helen, 45
Wilson Sporting Goods Company, 45–46
Wimbledon, 42, 45–46, 60, 63–64, 107, 110, 152–153, 166, 179
Wingfield, Major Walter Clopton, 42
Winn, William "Billy", 5, 70–72, 78
Woods, R.C., 29
Woods, Tiger, 174
World Tennis, 136
Wright, Walter Livingston, 23
Wright, William H., 43

Xavier University, 46

Young, Andrew "Andy", 152
Young, Donald, 162
Young, Houston G., 20